THE ART OF SELF
EMPOWERMENT

Practical Strategies to rise above Criticism and
Control to Reclaim your Self-Esteem

By

G.R. Stintzi

First Paperback Edition November 2024

ISBN 979-8-9919139-3-5 (Hard Cover)

Published by G.R. Stintzi

Contents

INTRODUCTION

Welcome to the world of self-empowerment, where we learn to stop handing out VIP passes to the judgments, opinions, and drama of others. You know that feeling when you accidentally step in gum? It's sticky and annoying, and you'd rather avoid it altogether. Well, the unsolicited opinions of others can feel a lot like that gum—unpleasant and hard to shake off. This book is your trusty guide to navigating through life's sticky situations, teaching you that you don't need to give power to the critic in the back row or the drama queens running rampant in your life. Grab your favorite snack, cozy up, and let's dive into the art of shrugging off those judgmental vibes like they're just pesky flies buzzing around your picnic. Your journey to empowerment starts now—minus the sticky mess! You find yourself scrolling through social media, surrounded by images of picture-perfect lives, feeling envy gnawing at your self-esteem. Yet instead of succumbing to the seductive allure of comparison, you choose to pause and let out a laugh at the absurdity of it all.

You recall when you spilled coffee on your shirt right before a big meeting. Instead of feeling embarrassed, you embraced the gaffe and shared the story, turning it into a humorous anecdote everyone enjoyed. Recognizing moments like these unlocks a pathway to self-acceptance that thrives on authenticity and joy.

You embrace your quirks, knowing that your unique experiences and abilities create a rich tapestry that shapes who you are.

-Learn practical strategies to reflect on your big and small achievements.

-Create humor-infused narratives that shift the focus from failure to growth.

-Build a supportive community that celebrates your authentic self, fostering deeper connections.

-Mastering the fine art of boundary-setting with style

-Learn to identify the pesky critics in your life—both the loud ones and the sneaky ones hiding behind sweet smiles

-Teach you how to bounce back from those dreaded backhanded compliments and snide remarks

-Discover practical, actionable steps to elevate your self-esteem, all while chuckling at the absurdity of life's little critiques.

Get ready to unleash your inner diva (or dude) and strut confidently through the minefield of negativity. With each turn of the page, you'll find yourself less bothered and more empowered, proving that laughter truly is the best defense against the critics of the world! Guiding you through life.

CHAPTER 1

CULTIVATING SELF-LOVE AMIDST CONTROL

Cultivating your independence amidst a controlling relationship is like trying to keep a triple-scoop ice cream cone upright and not on the ground on a blazing summer day—it's tricky. Or Imagine navigating a funhouse filled with mirrors reflecting not just your actual image but also distorted images that can chip away at your sense of self. And while it might feel like you're in an ongoing emotional tug-of-war with a smooth-talking champion of guilt-tripping and passive-aggressive remarks, your triumph comes when you learn to spot these subtle and not-so-subtle tactics from a mile away. Picture yourself as a radar expert for stealthy attacks on your self-worth—a role you didn't apply for but one you'll ace in style.

In this chapter, we dive headfirst into recognizing and addressing controlling relationship behaviors. Think of your individuality as a delicate souffle, easily deflated by poorly timed aggression or honey-disguised criticism. Here, you'll find strategies to navigate emotionally manipulative partnerships with the grace of an Olympic figure skater. Forget about surrendering your autonomy—this journey is about reclaiming your space and fortifying your boundaries. You'll discover methods to transform shaky connections into harmonious exchanges. By observing patterns and realizing when someone is playing a strategic game with your emotions, you become the master of your narrative.

Together, we'll explore tales of everyday triumphs, analyzing personal anecdotes where setting boundaries produced unexpected waves of respect and relief. Seize this opportunity for self-reflection and understand that identifying your triggers is akin to paying attention to the compass that navigates your life's journey. With newfound clarity, healthier decision-making, steering you toward sunshine rather than storm clouds.

Recognizing and Addressing Controlling Behaviors

As we dive into self-empowerment within relationships, it's crucial to recognize those subtle control tactics that can sneak in and compromise your individualism. Picture this: you're in the middle of a conversation with a friend or partner, and suddenly, you feel an inexplicable guilt for something trivial, like choosing a dinner spot. That's the art of guilt-tripping at play—a gentle yet firm tug at your conscience, making you question your decisions. Guilt-tripping often manifests as comments that suggest disappointment or martyrdom, leading you to second-guess your choices. Similarly, passive-aggressive behavior—those sarcastic remarks or backhanded compliments—can erode your confidence over time, leaving you tiptoeing around interactions to avoid another round of cryptic jabs.

Recognizing these subtle forms of control is akin to detecting a faint but persistent background noise in a crowded room—it takes practice and acute awareness. When you start noticing these patterns, you can see when your independence is being nudged aside. Imagine your self-worth as a tiny fortress; these behaviors sneak in like termites, slowly weakening the structure from within. You can start patching the walls and reclaiming your space by understanding them.

Next, let's talk about differentiating healthy connections from overtly manipulative ones. In relationships grounded in trust and respect, disagreements are resolved through open discussions and mutual understanding. But when manipulation slithers in, so do threats and intimidation. These aren't bold and immediate but instead a creeping escalation. Maybe it starts with a veiled threat of withdrawing affection or support if you don't act a certain way. Such tactics may initially appear as isolated events but often become habitual if unchecked.

To truly grasp this, think of a garden—healthy relationships are like nurturing plants with sunlight and water. At the same time, manipulation is akin to choking weeds that stifle growth with their shadowy creep. If you experience more fear than comfort from a relationship and if discussions end with you feeling coerced or belittled, it might be time to check the label: 'Caution, Manipulation Ahead.'

Recognizing patterns rather than viewing incidents in isolation is essential in addressing more profound issues. A manipulative person may repeat certain behaviors with strategic regularity—one day cajoling with sweetness and "It will never happen again" Then the subsequent deployment of anger to get their way. It's like watching someone play chess, moving pieces with intent even when their strategy isn't apparent until later. Observing these patterns provides clarity in assessing what is seemingly 'how things are' versus what's actively harming your mental space.

Now, pause and invite a moment of self-reflection. Often, our internalized messages—the narratives constructed by past experiences and societal conditioning—can blur our judgment of current situations. Are you tolerating manipulation because you've been subtly coached to equate love with putting others first, always? Or perhaps external validation has become so crucial that existing in its absence feels impossible. You gain clarity and control over your decisions by examining these emotional responses.

Reflect on a time when you felt empowered—what was different then? It's like looking at your life's highlight reel to pinpoint what environments allowed you to thrive independently.

You can better navigate healthier decision-making paths by understanding your triggers and reactions. It's akin to upgrading the radar guiding your ship, ensuring you're heading toward shining horizons rather than stormy seas.

Recounting personal anecdotes, such as remembering moments when you've set boundaries and stuck to them, offers perspective. Perhaps there was a situation where standing firm brought unexpected respect or relief. Sharing these narratives bolsters your resolve and reinforces the belief your individuality must not be sacrificed for companionship.

Establishing Boundaries and Nurturing Resilience

Picture this: you're on a roller coaster of emotional highs and lows in your relationship, often feeling like a sack of potatoes being tossed around. Enter the superhero of our tale—boundaries! Setting boundaries is akin to donning a cape of self-respect, shielding yourself from emotional turbulence while reinforcing your individuality. Imagine boundaries as an invisible fence. They protect your mental and physical space and signal to others where the no-go zones are. Healthy boundaries prevent sneaky trespassers from trampling over your peace, allowing you to flourish.

Now, let's dive into the different flavors of these boundary superheroes. First up, we have emotional boundaries, which act as a cushion for your feelings. They ensure you do not absorb every emotion thrown your way, like when Aunt Marge decided her drama was your responsibility. You can determine what emotions stick or slide off like water on a waxed car. Then there's the realm of physical boundaries—like your personal bubble wrap, safeguarding your physical space. Have you ever had that one friend who can't resist the urge to invade your circle? Physical boundaries set the guidelines for how close someone can get without triggering those inner alarm bells.

Time-related boundaries are next on the roster, ensuring you're not swamped with commitments that leave you gasping for air. Picture them as your calendar gatekeepers, allowing you to prioritize activities that nourish your soul rather than deplete it. This means being able to say "no" to yet another three-hour meeting that could've been an email. With these boundaries in place, your autonomy stands as firm as a stubborn cat stuck in your backyard oak tree.

Communicating these boundaries, however, requires an artistry akin to spinning a basketball on your finger—assertiveness. It's about clearly expressing what's okay and what's not, reducing misunderstandings faster than a magician pulling a rabbit out of a hat. When communicating, use language that demands respect but doesn't bulldoze anyone else's feelings. For instance, "I need time to recharge after work" conveys your needs without making it sound like everyone else is an energy vampire. Remember to be straightforward and calm; there's no need for elaborate justifications that make you feel like you're back in junior high algebra class.

Once you've set these boundaries, enforcing them becomes your full-time mission. Consistency is your ally here. It's like training a dog to sit—with enough repetition; people learn what flies and what doesn't. If someone crosses your boundaries, establish a consequence that matches their infraction level. It's the adult version of a timeout. However, recognize that some folks may not take well to this new, boundary-filled you. Stick to your guns because, ultimately, protecting your peace is non-negotiable (<i>Self Love Is Setting Boundaries - Retreat in the Pines</i>, 2023).

Let's not forget the vital art of nurturing self-compassion amidst all this boundary-setting. We often indulge in negative self-talk, like a broken record that refuses to shut up. Adopting positive affirmations is like swapping that annoying tune for the greatest hits of confidence. Tell yourself uplifting things like "I am enough" or "I deserve love," and repeat them until they're as ingrained as your favorite childhood jingle. Self-compassion means embracing your flaws and quirks rather than letting external criticism dictate your worth. Treat yourself with the kindness you'd show a small child convinced there's a monster under the bed.

As we wade through the stormy seas of life, cultivating self-love becomes our lighthouse, guiding us back to shore when negativity tries to capsize our ship. Creating a supportive environment involves surrounding yourself with buoyant people who remind you why you rock rather than anchors dragging you down. Find companions who celebrate your victories and help pick up the pieces during your blunders. A friend told me, "Though I gave everything to bring her joy, she made me feel less. Now, no matter what I do, the feeling lingers. Perhaps the only remedy is to find someone who can make me feel more." In the song EYE IN THE SKY, A few of the verses hit home:

[Verse 1]

Don't think sorry's quickly said
Don't try turning tables instead
You've taken lots of chances before
But I ain't gonna give anymore
Please don't ask me
That's how it goes
'Cause part of me knows what you're thinking

[Verse 2]

Don't say words you're gonna regret
Don't let the fire rush to your head
I've heard the accusation before
And I ain't gonna take any more
Believe me
The sun in your eyes
Made some of the lies worth believing

[Verse 3]

Don't leave false illusions behind
Don't cry, I ain't changin' my mind
So find another fool like before
'Cause I ain't gonna live anymore believin'
Some of the lies while all of the signs are deceiving

Engage in mindfulness practices that anchor you in the present moment, letting go of past mistakes or future worries, like releasing helium balloons into the sky. Mindfulness keeps you grounded so the waves of self-doubt don't wash you away. Incorporating simple breathing exercises or meditation into your routine is like giving your brain a vacation—a chance to relax and reboot.

Summary And Reflections

In this whirlwind chapter, we've taken a roller coaster ride through recognizing and confronting those sneaky little control tactics that can sometimes worm their way into relationships. Who knew choosing a dinner spot could somehow morph into a guilt-tripped expedition? We've unraveled the mysteries of passive-aggressive remarks, unveiling them for what they are: sly attempts to chip away at our confidence. By spotting these patterns, we empower ourselves to shore up our autonomy fortress, patching the walls and reclaiming our personal space.

We've also delved deep into the art of drawing boundaries—those invisible fences of self-respect that keep unwanted emotional intrusions at bay. Whether safeguarding your peace with emotional cushions or keeping your time commitments in check, it's about ensuring your mental garden gets just the right amount of sun without being overrun by weeds. With newfound assertiveness, you're not just surviving in the relationship jungle but thriving. Remember, with every boundary set and respected, you're saying "yes" to yourself, leaving manipulation in the dust and striding toward a healthier, happier you.

CHAPTER 2

UNDERSTANDING THE NOISE

Understanding the noise of external judgments is like trying to nap at a rock concert—no easy feat! The world never seems to run out of opinions, and we're all receivers whether we like it or not. From casual comments about our appearances to unsolicited advice on life choices, the constant chatter has a sneaky way of lodging itself into our minds. It's almost comical how such remarks, often tossed around lightly, can weigh heavily on our shoulders. Picture this: you're strutting down the street, feeling confident in your new outfit, when someone makes an offhand remark about a "bold choice." Suddenly, your confidence dips faster than a chicken nugget in ketchup. We find ourselves in a chaotic atmosphere where everyone believes they can dictate our identity, turning our lives into an endless search for approval.

In this chapter, we're diving into why these external judgments significantly impact self-esteem. We'll explore the origins of societal pressures, those unwritten rules that demand perfection and paradoxes. Imagine being urged to be assertive yet demure, wealthy but charitable; no wonder people feel like they're running in circles! We'll also examine how media intensifies the situation, creating unrealistic standards that distort our reality. And as if that wasn't enough, family values and peer pressure tag along, leaving us wondering if we'll ever measure up. But don't fret; amid this chaotic landscape, you'll find insights and empathy, offering hope for clarity amidst the contradictions. As we unravel these sources, we'll learn to question which standards truly align with us. Prepare to sift through the noise, embracing the beauty of individuality over societal expectations.

Origins Of Societal Pressures

In a world filled with voices telling us who we should be, it's a wonder anyone has time for self-discovery. Cultural norms are like an unwritten book of rules everyone seems to have read, but no one agrees. These norms create a checklist of qualities necessary for acceptance. They're confusing, much like assembling IKEA furniture without the instructions.

Cultural contradictions thrive because what's applauded in one setting can be scoffed at in another. For example, one might be urged to be assertive in professional life yet expected to be demure in personal relationships. This back-and-forth dance between different expectations leads to a whirlpool of confusion. When society's checklist demands that we be extroverted but also humble, wealthy, yet charitable, it's no surprise that people find themselves trapped in an endless loop of trying to meet these standards.

The media adds more fuel to the fire, as if cultural norms weren't enough. The portrayal of unrealistic standards in every media corner is like looking into a funhouse mirror that distorts reality to ridiculous proportions. Social media, in particular, acts as a highlight reel where everyone seems to be living their best lives. Of course, we often see carefully curated moments, not everyday existence's mundane or messy reality. The pressure to measure up to these illusions can lead to unhealthy comparisons and self-doubt, as scrolling through endless images of perfection paints a picture that rarely reflects actual reality.

Moreover, family values and critiques play a significant role in shaping our self-outlook. Many familial judgments stem from a place of love and concern, aiming to guide us toward a path deemed successful or proper by past generations. However, this well-meaning advice can sometimes feel stifling and damaging if it conflicts with one's ambitions or identity. It's like receiving a sweater you didn't ask for every holiday; each year, it's a different color but always one size too small. We carry childhood expectations into adulthood, leaving less room for growth when boxed into traditional roles or standards set by family members.

Another layer to tackle is peer pressure, which creates feelings of inadequacy that many grapple with despite the facade of confidence. Peers often experience similar insecurities, though this mutual struggle is seldom shared openly. It's like being stuck in a book club where everyone secretly hates the book but pretends otherwise. Peer groups can reinforce societal standards, making breaking free from comparing oneself to others difficult. The looming expectation to fit in can overshadow the awareness that peers are equally caught in the web of societal pressures.

Despite the noise created by cultural norms, media images, familial expectations, and peer pressure, understanding their origins can provide clarity and insight. Realizing that everyone is equally navigating this chaotic landscape allows for empathy and mutual support rather than competition and self-doubt.

The narrative we're fed about success and self-worth often overlooks the beauty in individuality. As we uncover the sources of societal expectations, it becomes vital to question which standards align with our true selves and discard those that don't. Embracing authenticity amidst contradictory social cues isn't just liberating—it's essential for mental health and genuine happiness.

Common Sources Of Judgment

Imagine you're sitting in a coffee shop, sipping your favorite hot beverage, when you suddenly catch snippets of the conversation at the following table. One friend is telling another how to wear more "appropriate" clothes for your age, and just like that, your self-esteem takes a nosedive. Welcome to the noisy world of external judgments, where your social circles can be your best cheerleaders and your harshest critics.

You see, our social circles are funny little places. They're filled with people who often love us dearly but sometimes pass along standards that can leave us wondering if we're good enough. Social identity theory suggests that these circles are not just about drinks and giggles; they shape our perception of ourselves as we strive to belong. So, what's the trick to enhancing self-esteem amid all this noise? It's learning to distinguish between constructive feedback and those anxiety-inducing offhand comments. A well-intended advice ("Hey, maybe try this new style for fun!") boosts your confidence rather than dragging it down like an overly critical voice from one's internal monologue. It's much easier to play that negative tape around and around in your head. It takes effort to play a positive loop.

Next up, let's talk about the beast known as workplace culture. Picture yourself at a team meeting, presenting your big idea. Your boss nods, but you feel deflated by a colleague's harsh critique. It's easy to misinterpret this as a measure of your worth or capability when, in reality, workplace feedback often reflects the culture of the environment itself. Most workplaces thrive on constant improvement, where critiques foster growth rather than diminish you. When you rethink this feedback as an opportunity for personal development, you're less likely to tie your self-worth to every raised eyebrow or email marked "urgent."

Now, let's journey into the online universe, a mixed bag of affection and animosity. Here, everyone seems to have a picture-perfect life, complete with never-ending vacations and gourmet breakfasts. But don't be fooled! Online personas are carefully curated creations designed to showcase the highlights, not the struggles. As tempting as measuring self-worth through likes and followers is, remember that what you see isn't always what you get. Instead, hone your skills in identifying supportive versus toxic interactions. Disengaging from negativity is not only a form of self-respect; it's a decisive stand for your mental peace.

Last but not least, let's address public perception overthinking—an exhausting game of "What will they think?" played in the theater of your mind. While it's natural to care about how others perceive us, placing too much weight on these opinions can undermine your confidence. Shifting focus from others' assessments to celebrating your unique qualities can lighten this burden tremendously. It invites you to engage in self-acceptance, shattering the shackles of public opinion.

Here's a quick recap: Social circles bring companionship and challenges to self-esteem, so it's critical to discern genuine guidance amidst passing judgments. In the workplace, criticism is viewed as a chance for growth, not a reflection of inadequacy. Navigate online waters wisely, recognizing the difference between authentic support and harmful interactions. Lastly, replace the habit of obsessing over public perceptions with the liberating act of self-acceptance. By doing so, you'll live more for personal contentment rather than external validation.

Effects On Personal Identity

Let's face it: the world comprises opinions, judgments, and unsolicited advice. We're all contestants on a never-ending reality show where everyone else has a say in our lives. But how much do these external judgments affect our self-perception and identity? Spoiler alert: quite a bit.

Starting with self-image, it's fascinating—and slightly terrifying—how easily external judgments can warp it. Have you ever noticed how a friend's casual remark about your outfit can leave you reconsidering your entire wardrobe? We often assign worth to these perceptions rather than holding onto our internal values. Imagine developing a filter that only lets positive, constructive criticism through while blocking out the noise. Our self-esteem would probably win an Olympic gold medal.

Now, let's dive into impostor syndrome—a sneaky little devil that thrives on comparisons. Picture this: you're scrolling through Instagram, seeing curated success stories from peers who seem to have it all figured out. Suddenly, you're questioning your talents, seeking validation from an outside audience that hardly knows the real you. However, many forget that nobody's life is as perfect as it appears online. Learning to appreciate these behind-the-scenes realities can be a first step toward defanging this beast called impostor syndrome. And here's a fun fact: those in higher positions likely feel the same way but won't readily admit it.

Conflicting messages sure know how to spark some wild identity crises. Society tells us to be unique, yet it also insists we fit neatly into predefined boxes. Talk about mixed signals! It's like being asked to dance in two different ways at once. This constant push and pull can make authenticity feel like finding a needle in a haystack. Wouldn't it be freeing to prioritize self-discovery over conforming to outdated definitions before they're even written down?

And speaking of liberation, there's unmatched freedom in embracing one's true self. Accepting who you genuinely are feels like shaking off heavy societal shackles. Once you begin acknowledging the absurdity of trying to please everyone, you'll unlock a sense of empowerment rooted in uniqueness. "Dare to be different," they say, for a good reason. Realizing that being unapologetically yourself is the most potent form of rebellion against societal pressures allows us to navigate life with newfound clarity and joy.

So, what's the takeaway here? External judgments are unavoidable; they're part and parcel of human interaction. However, recognizing their impact opens the door to understanding how they positively and negatively shape us. It's crucial to remember that behind every polished facade lies an imperfect human being trying to make sense of it all.

Building Self-Resilience

Navigating the noise of societal expectations can be quite the emotional rollercoaster, can't it? It's like trying to find your way in a maze with neon signs screaming for your attention. Never fear, though; we will explore how fostering resilience and reinforcing self-esteem can help us gracefully waltz through this chaos.

First, let's chat about self-awareness, our trusty flashlight in the dark corridors of life. Developing self-awareness is like discovering you've had an internal GPS all along. It helps spot those negative influences lurking around, just waiting to mess with your groove. For instance, have you ever noticed how some friends always have a comment or critique? They might mean well, but their words can seep into our minds, creating unwanted pressure. By fine-tuning your self-awareness, you start recognizing these patterns. It's like being able to tell the difference between genuine feedback and unsolicited advice from Aunt Karen at family gatherings—who has never really understood your fashion choices!

If you consider life a grand sitcom where everyone plays a role, supportive networks are your co-stars cheering you on. These people know the real you—the version of yourself that sometimes wears mismatched socks and loves quirky puns. Building and maintaining these networks is crucial because they enhance mental well-being and provide a soft landing when you trip over life's obstacles. When the world feels like it's trying out for a reality TV drama, the folks who love you reassure you of your authentic self, offering comfort without judgment.

Let's sprinkle in some self-compassion—think of it as the marshmallows in your hot chocolate. Practicing self-compassion means treating yourself with the tenderness you'd offer a dear friend. We've all seen those goofy cats on social media making epic fails yet remaining utterly adorable. Well, practicing self-compassion allows us to view our missteps with similar kindness. This gentle approach reduces the sting of external judgments and steers your focus toward personal growth and positivity. So next time you metaphorically spill milk, remember: you're still fabulous and not defined by the little slips.

Setting personal goals and values is like choosing what songs play on your life's playlist. Sure, external noises may try to distract you, but having clear goals ensures you bop along at your rhythm, undeterred by the clashing cymbals of judgment. Imagine your life as a movie. Wouldn't you rather be the director than an extra, lost in the background? Establishing personal goals directs your attention away from the hustle and bustle, letting you prioritize what truly satisfies your soul. Whether climbing the corporate ladder or mastering the ukulele, ensure those goals echo your values—not just what's trending on Twitter.

To foster resilience against societal pressures, remember that this journey isn't about dodging every hurdle flawlessly. It's about learning to embrace challenges with humor and grace. After all, life's path isn't neatly paved; sometimes, it's more like a quirky obstacle course. Each tumble allows you to grow stronger and more assured in your skin. Celebrate the small victories along the way, and don't forget to laugh—it's the best remedy for sticky situations.

Final Insights

In an age where we're all trying to juggle societal expectations like a circus performer with too many flaming torches, this chapter looks into how external judgments tend to crash-land onto our self-esteem. The pressure can feel relentless, whether from well-meaning family members attempting to control our lives or our social circles tossing critiques like confetti at a parade. And let's not forget the funhouse mirror effect of social media, which turns ordinary moments into glitzy highlights and leaves us scrolling through a fantasyland that rivals any blockbuster movie. Yet, amidst this chaos, understanding these influences allows us to take a step back and prioritize what's important—our own happiness and mental health.

This chapter invites us to use glasses of clarity and self-awareness to navigate this whirlwind of voices. With a touch of humor, it reminds us that not every piece of unsolicited advice needs to be taken to heart. Instead, it's about turning the volume down on the noisy opinions of others and tuning into our unique rhythm. By filtering out the white noise and learning to embrace our authentic selves, we discover that the secret to building self-esteem isn't hidden in hashtags or the number of likes but lies within our ability to laugh off the absurdity of trying to please everyone. In embracing who we are, we unlock a liberating path to resilience and joy, allowing us to dance through life confidently.

CHAPTER 3

LAUGHING AT THE CRITICS

Laughing at the critics is like wielding a secret weapon in the everyday battle against judgment and self-doubt. This approach turns stinging reviews and snide remarks into punchlines, turning life's unwelcome critiques into comedic opportunities. Instead of letting critiques cut deep, readers are invited to join a journey where humor acts as a buffer, transforming harsh words into harmless paper planes. The focus isn't on ignoring feedback but rather reimagining it through a lens of light-heartedness and resilience. This chapter begins by exploring the power of laughter as a robust defense mechanism, offering readers insights into how humor can become an ally during moments of vulnerability.

As the chapter unfolds, you'll dive into the mechanics of converting criticism into comedy gold, much like comedians who have mastered turning personal setbacks into laugh-worthy anecdotes. This was Rodney Dangerfield's whole comic routine that he made famous. (I get no RESPECT) Discover strategies for crafting humorous narratives that shift the balance of power away from external judgments, placing it firmly in your hands. Through relatable stories and practical advice, this chapter opens ways to use humor as a shield and a bridge toward deeper connections with others. As you learn to laugh at yourself, societal expectations become lighter, and the journey toward self-acceptance transforms into joy and camaraderie. Whether it's learning to view criticism as a source of amusement or shared laughter, this chapter promises to blend humor with empowerment in meaningful ways.

The Power Of Laughter

Laughter often acts like a shield against life's harshest critics, providing a witty comeback and a genuine physiological response that softens the blow. When we laugh, our bodies release endorphins, those delightful little chemicals that dance through our brains, lifting our spirits and vanishing stress as swiftly as a magician hides a coin. This natural stress-relief mechanism can dim the intensity of criticism, making negative words less like arrows and more like paper planes veering off into harmless directions.

Imagine receiving a particularly cutting remark at work or on social media. Consider wielding humor as your ally instead of allowing it to fester in your heart. Humor shifts your focus away from the sting of judgment, transforming the daunting mountain of criticism into a light-hearted molehill. By laughing off negativity, you place yourself in a position of strength where outside opinions neither bruise nor define you. It's about turning a potential tragedy into a comedy, where you're both the heroic protagonist and the quick-witted storyteller.

Moreover, crafting a humorous narrative around criticism is akin to flipping the script of your own story. You're no longer the victim of biting comments; you're the cunning author who twists adversity into amusing anecdotes. Creating such narratives allows individuals to reclaim their personal stories, ensuring others' bleak interpretations do not trap them. When you laugh at your faults or missteps, you take charge of the tale, leaving critics fumbling for relevance in the audience. This shift in narrative control disarms critics effectively, like pulling the plug from a loud radio playing head-banging noise.

Research enthusiastically backs up this comedic approach to resilience. Scientific studies have found that humor fortifies mental health, bolstering resilience to challenges (Lonczak, 2020). Engaging in laughter isn't just good for warding off unwanted criticisms and fostering more profound connections with those around us. Shared laughter turns acquaintances into allies, making the world seem far less foreboding and more of a collaborative stage for shared levity.

Consider how humor's role extends beyond individual empowerment to social tendencies. A well-timed joke can be the olive branch that bridges differences, encouraging openness and vulnerability among peers. This communal aspect of laughter builds networks of support that help cushion us against critical assaults. When friends gather to share a chuckle, they're not just enjoying a moment; they're constructing invisible walls of camaraderie strong enough to repel negativity.

Creating a humorous narrative might sound like an intricate art form, but it's entirely accessible. Try viewing a critical comment as the foundation of a joke. Observe its absurdity, exaggerate its flaws, and find the irony embedded within. The next time someone points out an embarrassing slip-up, picture yourself performing a stand-up routine where you spin the incident into comedy gold. This approach lightens your emotional load and arms you with a powerful tool for future encounters.

Indeed, scientific perspectives indicate that humor cultivates robustness in mental health, characterized by enhanced resilience and fortified social bonds (Pistoia, 2022). Humor becomes a shared language spoken among those who understand its nuances and relish its ability to connect people on a deeper level. These connections morph into a tight-knit community, shielding individuals from the isolating effects of external judgments.

The beauty of humor lies in its versatility; it can be employed to deflect personal insecurities and confront societal expectations. By embracing humor, you're choosing to stand tall amidst the clamor of differing voices. You're cultivating emotional well-being through a lens that finds joy in the mundane and laughter in the unexpected.

When harnessed thoughtfully, laughter aligns with positive coping mechanisms—a valuable defense against the shadows of doubt and criticism. It's crucial, however, to underscore that not all humor is created equal. Aligning with positive forms of humor—uplifting rather than tearing down—maximizes the benefits while minimizing potential harm.

Turning Criticism Into Comedy

Sometimes, life feels like one never-ending episode of a reality show where you're the main character everyone loves to hate. Yet, what if you could transform those critical moments into the highlight reel of a stand-up comedy special? It might sound counterintuitive, but finding humor in hostile situations can be an unexpected yet incredibly effective way to reclaim control over your emotions and foster empowerment. Many times, the one person at work who is gifted in one-liners and witty comebacks is usually looked up to with respect.

Consider the world of comedians. They seem to have mastered this art of turning life's misfortunes into laugh-out-loud moments. When you can laugh at something that initially seemed hurtful or embarrassing, it loses its power over you. Think about Robin Williams or Rosanne Barr, whose comedic acts often dove deep into personal struggles, weaving laughter through narratives that society might typically deem too personal or tragic for such treatment. By confronting societal judgments with humor, they defied expectations and brought audiences along on a journey of cathartic release.

Creating a comedy arsenal is not just about collecting punchlines; it's about embracing life's absurdities. Compiling humorous anecdotes from personal experiences allows you to see the lighter side of what might otherwise weigh heavily on your heart. This creative outlet is a confidence booster and a springboard for personal expression. Start small. Keep a journal where you jot down everyday mishaps—like when you tripped on air while wearing your brand-new high heels or when your pet decided to chase his tail was best performed during a serious Zoom meeting. Before long, you'll look forward to capturing these moments, reframing them as funny instead of frustrating.

Sharing these funny takes on criticism with others does more than lighten your load—it builds protective communities around you. In laughing together, we create stronger bonds than the criticisms aiming to pull us down. Imagine a group of friends cracking up over their collective awkwardness or a family sharing stories about everything that hilariously went wrong during the last reunion. These shared experiences nurture a sense of belonging and understanding. Engaging others in laughter about your blunders invites them into a space devoid of judgment, where everyone is human, flawed, and remarkably relatable.

Finding the funny in the harsh requires looking at criticism not as a wall but as a door to creativity and connection. Here are a few guidelines to get you started: First, identify situations that sting—those moments when you felt judged or inadequate. Pause and ask yourself, "What's so absurd about this?" Maybe it's the irony of how your supposedly 'unfit' body managed to outlast others in a race, or perhaps it's about receiving unsolicited advice from people who haven't figured things out themselves. Next, permit yourself to exaggerate these moments when recounting them. A slight embellishment can add humor without distorting the truth. Finally, share these stories with trusted circles, inviting their laughter to become the balm that soothes your bruises.

Remember, humor isn't about diminishing the seriousness of real issues but rather about offering a fresh perspective. According to research highlighted by Tallulah Knill Allen (2024), humor can act as a healing force, transforming how individuals view their challenges. The essence lies in balance—using laughter as a tool for reflection rather than avoidance.

By approaching life's judgments with humor, you are not just playing defense but flipping the script entirely. Suddenly, the critic becomes the catalyst for creativity, and the jeering crowd morphs into an audience ready for your next punchline. Whether you're channeling personal experiences into a night at an open mic, penning a light-hearted blog post, or simply sharing a good laugh with a friend over coffee, remember that every wisecrack is a reclaiming of your narrative.

Relatable Anecdotes

There's something almost universally comforting in the realization that everyone, at some point, has experienced the burning sensation of embarrassment. Consider the time Sally, a college student, found herself giving a speech when suddenly, her mind blanked, and all she could do was chuckle awkwardly and say, "Well, this is awkward!" Instead of succumbing to panic, she leaned into humor— her laughter resonated throughout the room, transforming an embarrassing moment into an endearing and oddly memorable one. This story reminds us that facing judgment through humor is a personal coping mechanism and a universal balm.

The magic of laughter lies in its ability to stitch together the common threads of human experience. Take, for instance, the legendary actress Lucille Ball, who turned countless blunders into comedic gold on screen and taught generations the art of laughing at oneself. Reading about such figures inspires us to reframe our narratives, using humor as a powerful tool to soften the blow of criticism while fostering self-acceptance. Understanding that even those we admire have stumbled and laughed off mistakes paints a picture where vulnerability becomes an asset rather than a liability.

Humor in storytelling goes beyond mere entertainment; it embodies authenticity and courage. When we share our stories laced with humor, we allow others to glimpse our true selves. This embrace of authenticity turns what might be viewed as weaknesses into strengths. There's an art to weaving humor into narratives, where timing, tone, and self-awareness play pivotal roles. By mastering this art, individuals can craft stories that resonate deeply, inviting listeners or readers to join them in laughter and reflection. Whether it's recounting a wardrobe malfunction during a crucial meeting or tripping during a romantic date, these tales transform vulnerabilities into relatable anecdotes, celebrating the messiness of life with a lighthearted touch.

Creating a network of individuals who embrace humor as a coping mechanism nurtures a sense of community. Imagine being part of a group chat where the motto is simple: when in doubt, laugh it out. Such networks can become vital support systems, offering shared experiences and a safe space where judgment is met with good-natured humor instead of criticism. Within these circles, people learn how to laugh at their hiccups and support others in doing the same, reinforcing collective resilience. This communal approach reinforces that no one stands alone in their struggles or triumphs, fostering solidarity and empathy.

Guidelines can be invaluable in this narrative journey, especially in cultivating the art of storytelling with humor and forming supportive communities. For storytelling, one must remember that humor should never come at the expense of unkindness or disrespect of others. It's about finding the balance between teasing oneself and maintaining dignity. Likewise, developing a supportive humor network involves setting boundaries that ensure all humor is inclusive, respectful, and constructive.

These guidelines act as anchors, ensuring that humor remains a tool for building resilience and not a weapon for unintended harm.

As we explore the idea of using humor to navigate judgment and enhance self-acceptance, we find that the beauty of these stories often lies in their simplicity and relatability. They are reminders that life's path is riddled with stumbles and slips, yet each provides a unique opportunity to rethink our approach to criticism. Humor doesn't erase the hurdles but offers a perspective that makes them more manageable and less intimidating. Through personal stories, influential anecdotes, or shared networks, laughter bridges the individual to the broader world, encouraging everyone to embrace their imperfections and potential.

Using Laughter To Build Connection

Laughter, as simple as it sounds, wields extraordinary power. When shared, it can bring us closer together, fostering connections that transcend superficial critiques and judgments. In a world where criticism can often feel unyielding, sharing laughter becomes not just a form of entertainment but a vital tool for building more robust, more resilient relationships.

It starts with the concept of camaraderie. Picture a group caught in a fit of giggles over a mutual joke or amusing incident. Laughing together creates a bond that tells everyone involved they are part of something bigger. This is where humor acts as a social glue, encouraging a sense of unity and mitigating judgmental attitudes. People find common ground, creating an atmosphere where laughter precedes the differences that might otherwise divide them.

An insightful study at the University of North Carolina highlighted this phenomenon by demonstrating how shared laughter can increase feelings of similarity and connection between individuals (Suttie, 2017). Participants who laughed together felt

26

more alike and showed a heightened desire for further interaction. Laughter signals that we see the world similarly, wiping away barriers and drawing us into each other's lives.

Once we establish this supportive circle through humor, something remarkable happens — external criticisms become quieter, mere whispers against the backdrop of shared joy. Humor invites vulnerability and openness, essential elements for forging deep connections. When people engage in humorous exchanges, they reveal glimpses of authenticity, allowing others to see past their defenses. In this vulnerable state, criticisms lose their sting, overshadowed by the warmth of shared laughter.

This bonding experience isn't fleeting; it lays the groundwork for enduring relationships. Humor within interactions becomes a protective shield against judgment's isolating effects. It nurtures a safe space where individuals can express themselves freely without fear of being torn down by external opinions. Consider how long-term couples often cherish inside jokes that have developed over time. These bits of shared humor are memories and testimonies of a relationship's strength, providing resilience during challenging times.

Moreover, studies suggest that humor plays a crucial role in relationship longevity. For instance, older couples reportedly use humor to convey tenderness and lessen conflict, demonstrating its importance even decades into a partnership (<i>Why It Takes Humor to Sustain a Long-Term Relationship | Psyche Ideas</i>, n.d.). This highlights the protective nature of humor against the relentless tide of criticism and negativity, proving its worth beyond mere amusement.

For those struggling with societal expectations and self-esteem issues, embracing shared laughter offers a relatable yet practical approach to self-improvement. By seeking opportunities to laugh with others, whether friends, family, or colleagues, individuals invite a sense of community that inherently diminishes judgment.

A quick-witted comment at a meeting can break the tension, making the workplace more collaborative and less critical. Similarly, friendships flourish when punctuated by humor, transforming casual acquaintances into stalwart allies ready to fend off unfair criticisms together.

In practice, incorporating laughter into daily routines doesn't require grand gestures. Simple, everyday moments provide ample opportunity for shared humor. Watching a comedy show with loved ones, engaging in light-hearted banter during a meal, or recalling funny stories from the past all contribute to the fabric of shared experiences that bolster relationships. Importantly, these moments remind us that amidst life's hardships, there is always room for joy and connection.

Reflecting on Sara Algoe's research, it becomes evident that shared laughter should be a deliberate choice in our interactions. Just as we plan meetings and deadlines, we can consciously create spaces for humor, ensuring it becomes an integral part of our relationship-building efforts. While individual laughter certainly uplifts spirits, participating in comedic exchanges amplifies our sense of belonging, fortifying us against criticism's harsh tones.

Summary And Reflections

Laughter, as we've explored, isn't just a breather from life's pressures; it's a formidable tool that flips the script on criticism. By harnessing humor, we transform biting comments into punchlines, deflecting negativity with ease and panache. Every giggle, chuckle, and snort is a step towards reclaiming your narrative, shielding you even in the face of harsh judgments. Whether you're comparing your latest blunder to a stand-up routine or finding absurdity in criticisms, each moment of levity builds a resilient self-image. With humor, you're not just surviving external judgments; you're thriving beyond them, turning even the sharpest critiques into sources of amusement.

But laughter's true magic lies in its ability to connect people. Shared hilarity builds a community where judgments lose their bite, overshadowed by camaraderie and joy. A simple inside joke or a shared laugh at a memory strengthens bonds, making criticism seem like mere background noise. Think of humor as the glue holding relationships together—an antidote for isolation. As you embark on this comedic journey, remember that every clever quip and funny story adds a layer of protection against societal pressures. So, embrace the absurdities, gather your friends, and let laughter lead to a more confident and connected you.

CHAPTER 4

DETECTING DRAMA AND DETACHING

Detecting drama is like spotting a rainbow trout in a clear mountain stream—often tricky but always rewarding once you master the technique. In our bustling lives, it can be easy to get swept up in unnecessary theatrics, whether it's a heated exchange over who last left the lights on or diving headfirst into someone else's emotional whirlwind. Drama seems to have an all-access pass to our everyday interactions, thriving on miscommunication and sweeping us into roles we never auditioned for. But imagine breaking free from this exhausting loop, preserving your energy for things that truly matter. It's about learning to recognize these melodramatic moments before they pull you under, much like spotting storm clouds on the horizon while you enjoy a sunny picnic.

This chapter revolves around recognizing the culprit behind the curtains and learning to step away with grace and humor intact. You'll explore how to identify the telltale signs of drama-laden pit stops—those frequent misunderstandings and guilt trips that seem to crop up out of nowhere. Anyone can flip between victim, rescuer, and persecutor faster than a channel-surfing spree during commercials. This book's journey offers a fresh perspective on why we fall prey to such scripting and how to gracefully dodge the allure of reenacting soap opera theatrics in real life. With a light-hearted touch, you'll uncover strategies to dodge those banana peel moments, where well-meaning involvement morphs into energy-draining entanglements. Consider this your backstage pass to finding ways to reclaim your emotional space, ensuring that your stage is set for genuine connection rather than perpetual encore performances of life's little dramas.

Recognizing Toxic Drama

Navigating the whirlwind of toxic drama in encounters and relationships can be as thrilling—and terrifying—as trying to tame a wild Mustang. But fear not! It's about understanding the cycles that sweep us up and how we can dodge them with grace and humor. Enter the Drama Triangle, a concept that dramatically unveils the roles of victim, rescuer, and persecutor in our social narratives. Sounds like role-playing. You bet! And it's often happening without lines or scripts.

Imagine this: you're caught in a heated argument with a friend. Suddenly, you feel like a victim trapped in their oppressive tirade (cue the tiny violin). Emotions swirl; before you know it, you've adopted a defensive stance, casting the other person as the ruthless persecutor. Ah, but here's where things get interesting—you might also seamlessly slip into being the noble rescuer, swooping in with unsolicited advice, thinking you have just the proper remedy for everyone's troubles. This is your cue to recognize that, much like an impromptu improv game, none of these roles are fixed, and anyone can find themselves wearing a different hat depending on the day's drama forecast. A political opinion exchange, anyone!

So, what's the harm in these whimsical roles, you ask? When we're typecast—deliberately or unconsciously—into one of these parts, we bind ourselves in patterns that drain more emotional energy than a drama marathon on streaming TV. The allure of these familiar roles is strong, pulling us into repetitive scenarios where personal power dims as dramatically as the lights after a villain's monologue. For instance, continually playing the victim may prevent you from recognizing your virtues. In contrast, the rescuer might feel the weight of carrying others' burdens, feeding the ego but starving the self—it's a trade-off not worthy of Oscars.

Let's don our detective hats and spotlight patterns that ensnare us in drama-laden episodes. Often, these situations manifest as a series of "if only" statements, which become the soundtrack to our life's drama play. "If only they understood me," whispers the victim. "If only I could fix everything," echoes the rescuer. This pattern becomes clear when we note repeated instances where interactions devolve into blame games or rescue missions instead of mutual understanding and growth. Recognizing these loops can be the first step to cutting ties with the melodrama. Consider this a chance to rewrite the script where everyone can win Best Supporting Actor without needing support.

No drama narrative is complete without identifying red flags that scream 'drama ahead!' Picture this: frequent misunderstandings, excessive guilt-tripping, or sudden shifts in mood akin to plot twists nobody saw coming. These are fuel signs of interactions soaked in drama rather than genuine connection. You might notice someone trying to steer conversations towards their past sufferings to garner sympathy, or maybe there's an overenthusiastic 'helper' providing solutions without invitations. Recognizing these cues can give you the foresight to sidestep unnecessary entanglements and save your emotional energy for a real crisis—like deciding what to eat for dinner.

In daily interactions, we inadvertently step into these roles like tripping over a child's toy—a little embarrassing and entirely avoidable once you know it's there. Imagine you're at work, dealing with a colleague who constantly collapses under pressure. You rush in, channeling your inner superhero, ready to rescue them from deadlines and dilemmas. However, in doing so, you reinforce their reliance on others instead of teaching them resilience. Play this scenario to yourself and spot whether you're nurturing growth or fueling the cyclical fire.

Here's a guideline to help avoid stepping on the proverbial banana peel: next time you sense the gravitational pull of the drama universe, pause and reflect. Is the interaction fostering collaboration and empowerment, or does it feel more like a merry-go-round of recurring themes? Are you enabling dependency under the guise of helping? Identifying these tells can inspire you to foster healthier dynamics—perhaps by adopting a more empowering alternative where everyone mutually takes charge of their role.

Ultimately, disengaging from the drama web is not about slapping labels or pointing fingers, though that sometimes sounds delightful. It's about recognizing the actors and scenes within the theatrical production of life and choosing not to audition for any role in the Drama Triangle. Real empowerment lies in stepping out of the narrative to embrace a storyline where personal power is celebrated and shared genuinely. Whether it's through humor, insight, or simply taking a breather to look back and laugh, understanding these roles helps preserve your most valuable resources: your emotional energy and capacity for self-love.

Practical Detachment Strategies

In the complex tapestry of human relationships, there comes a time when we must become emotional tailors, skillfully threading our way through the drama to ensure that our emotional garments remain intact. It's complicated; sometimes, we wrestle with a three-headed hydra of emotions, expectations, and societal pressures. But fear not! With some humorous insights and practical techniques, stepping away from toxic behaviors and environments can be refreshing.

First, let's discuss the power of establishing physical and emotional boundaries. Imagine yourself as a noble knight defending your kingdom, except instead of a sword; you wield the art of saying "no" like a seasoned diplomat. Boundaries are your castle walls, offering protection against the siege of unnecessary drama. When you set these boundaries, you tell the world, "I value my peace more than your chaos." Saying no without guilt is liberating. It's okay to decline that invitation to criticize or complain; after all, who needs more stress when binge-watching the latest show with a tub of popcorn is much more appealing?

Moving forward, picture mindful disengagement as the ultimate magic trick—now you see the drama and don't. Visualization methods can help transport you to a calm meadow, perhaps surrounded by unicorns gently grazing. Mindful disengagement isn't just about closing your eyes and pretending chaos doesn't exist; it's about acknowledging the noise and choosing not to participate in the discord. Visualizing serene scenarios creates mental distance from triggering situations, like changing the channel on life's more obnoxious reality shows.

Of course, it's essential to find and nurture supportive influences. Uplifting friends are like rare gemstones glistening amid the rough terrain of life's challenges. They are the enthusiastic cheerleaders in your parade, waving pom-poms made of encouragement and kindness. Identifying these precious souls and nurturing those relationships is critical. Remember, you become the average of your five closest friends, so choose wisely! And if you discover that some companions lean more towards melodrama than meaningful dialogue, it might be time to expand your social circle.

Now, about those toxic environments—ever notice how they tend to suck the oxygen right out of the room? Just like walking into a crowded elevator where someone's wearing too much cologne, such spaces can feel overwhelmingly stifling. Creating physical distance can provide much-needed relief. Sometimes, it means stepping back, just walking away and disengaging. You can breathe easier and reassess your surroundings, like finding a quiet corner at a bustling party where you can recharge and sip your drink peacefully.

The beauty of these techniques lies in their simplicity and practicality. There is no need for elaborate rituals or expensive retreats—instead, these small, everyday actions empower us to reclaim our emotional sovereignty. Sometimes, relinquishing control feels daunting, but remember: you're not responsible for orchestrating every interaction. Humans are unpredictable creatures, much like cats deciding whether they want affection or solitude at any given moment.

A crucial element in this journey is recognizing your limits. Emotional energy, contrary to popular belief, isn't an infinite resource. Think of it more like a cellphone battery; if you constantly run multiple apps (or listen to endless complaints), you'll drain it faster than a teenager at a social media convention. By establishing clear boundaries and opting out of non-essential dramas, you conserve this precious energy for what truly matters—your growth, your happiness, and occasionally indulging in the guilty pleasure of reality TV (because, let's face it, sometimes other people's drama is entertaining, as long as it's not your own).

Ultimately, emotionally detaching from toxic behaviors and environments is akin to fine-tuning a radio dial—adjusting until you find the frequency that plays your song without static interference. Embrace the power of 'no' to avoid drama, practice mindful disengagement to keep serenity within reach, and seek out those uplifting influences that make life more prosperous and rewarding.

Preserving Emotional Energy

Do you feel like your emotional energy is being drained faster than a smartphone battery during a Netflix binge? Welcome to the club! But unlike your phone, you can't just plug yourself in and return to 100%. Suppose you've ever wondered why you feel exhausted after seemingly mundane interactions. In that case, it might be time to conduct an energy audit—a fascinating dive into understanding where all your emotional energy gets spent.

An energy audit isn't about sitting in a room full of incense sticks, though you can do that if it helps. It's more of a reflective exercise. Picture yourself as an accountant who's not working on numbers but emotions. Consider this: tracking what drains or boosts your mood over a week could reveal a lot. Like realizing that your coffee addiction isn't just about needing caffeine—it's also about getting away from Carol in Accounting, who seems to have mistaken your patience for interest in her daily drama saga. Just knowing this can prevent you from losing hours of what could be productive, or at least enjoyable, time.

Now, let's move on to recognizing personal triggers and celebrating victories over past engagements with drama. It's like looking back at those embarrassing school photos and finally appreciating how far you've come—without the braces and questionable fashion choices. Triggers can be sneaky, sometimes disguised as well-meaning friends or family members who don't understand the art of giving constructive criticism. Remember when Aunt Judy pointed out every possible flaw during Thanksgiving dinner? Yeah, that's a trigger. The key here is to identify these emotional landmines early so you can tiptoe around them or, better yet, disarm them altogether.

So, what's next after identifying these pesky triggers? Victory laps, metaphorically speaking. Acknowledge moments where you successfully walked away from unnecessary drama like a boss. In the past, you might have engaged in a heated debate with a neighbor over the height of their fence, but at present, you shrug it off with the grace of someone who knows when to pick their battles. Recognizing these triumphs builds confidence and reinforces the idea that you control your emotional landscape—not the other way around.

Let's talk self-care now—like fun self-care, not just scrolling through Instagram or TikTok. We're diving into stuff that genuinely recharges you. Perhaps it's dancing like no one's watching (because they're judging anyway), painting abstract masterpieces that even Picasso would squint at, or sofa marathons watching Netflix. Whatever floats your boat, as long as it brings joy and peace. The point is to indulge in activities that feed your soul without leaving you feeling guilty or obliged. Imagine turning your downtime into "uptime" by doing things that replenish instead of deplete.

And while we're on joyful indulgences, let's address cultivating positive accountability. Imagine sharing your recharging rituals with a friend who won't judge you for binging another cooking show despite never actually cooking anything. When you create shared experiences with like-minded allies, you're not just adding social spice to your life; you're forming a network of support that silently says, "I got your back." It's almost like a secret club where everyone vows to enrich each other's lives without playing the drama card. So, initiate mutual check-ins where laughing until your sides hurt is the main objective, and carrying each other's burdens feels light.

While you're banking on comedy and camaraderie, remember to sprinkle a little compassion for yourself along the way. Sometimes, you'll slip, engage more than you'd like in unwarranted drama, or forget to say no when your energy reserves scream for mercy. That's alright. Look at it this way: if we didn't fail occasionally, sitcoms wouldn't exist, and boy, do we love those! Laugh at the absurdity of life whenever possible because laughter doesn't just heal; it gives perspective. We learn, adapt, and eventually master the art of gracefully navigating through emotional minefields without letting outside chaos dictate our internal peace.

The Absurdity Of Drama

Let's face it—unnecessary drama can be as absurd as a sitcom plot. We often find ourselves stuck in melodramatic situations that, in hindsight, feel more like a comedy of errors than anything else. So, why not use humor to highlight the ridiculousness of engaging in such theatrics? Picture this: you're at work, and suddenly, there's a hullabaloo over who drank the last cup of coffee. The tension rises, voices escalate, eyebrows furrow—only to discover a fresh pot quietly brewing on the adjoining counter. If this were shown on TV, the canned laughter would echo around the office.

Injecting humor into everyday drama scenarios helps us see their absurdity. We've all been caught up in a spiraling argument about something trivial. Imagine turning these moments into stand-up material, poking fun at how the small stuff majorly derailed our day. "And there we were, debating for ten minutes whether it's pronounced 'tomato' or 'tomato,' only to agree that neither of us likes salads!" Laughing at our dramatic tendencies allows us to step back, view the situation objectively, and let go of the unnecessary emotional baggage.

Reflecting on past experiences, we've often encountered moments where the drama seemed overwhelming, yet in retrospect, they offer valuable lessons wrapped in comedic gold. Think back to your first breakup. It felt like the end of the world, complete with melancholic playlists and ice cream binges. Fast forward a few years, and you realize the best part wasn't the sulking—it was the new detective series on Tubi you discovered while sulking. These reflections provide insights into navigating future dramas with a lighter heart and a chuckle.

Light-hearted anecdotes serve as gentle nudges, encouraging us to question whether getting swept up in drama is worthwhile. Imagine a friend retelling an epic tale of mistakenly wearing mismatched socks to a client meeting. The horror! The embarrassment! Yet, in the grand scheme of things, it is not monumental at all. Such stories remind us of life's unpredictability and reassure us that laughing off minor blunders is far healthier than wallowing in them. When we share these narratives, we say, "Hey, I'm human, too. Let's laugh it off together."

Encouraging readers to laugh at themselves and their situations isn't just about self-deprecation; it's about empowerment through levity. Acknowledging our quirks and susceptibility to drama makes us more forgiving of others' failings. This shared vulnerability fosters connections, making it easier for everyone to dismiss the ludicrous elements of drama instead of fanning its flames. Picture a group of friends reminiscing about the ridiculous arguments they've had, like which way the toilet paper should hang. They all know the answer isn't the point—their laughter at the absurdity is.

We sometimes need to question why we engage in these dramatic escapades repeatedly. Is it because we've been conditioned to find excitement in chaos? Are we subconsciously yearning for the attention it generates? This reflective questioning is crucial. While it's essential to accommodate some natural degree of drama, habitual engagement in needless drama drains our emotional reserves. Realizing the futility of these theatricals enables us to conserve energy for pursuits that uplift rather than drain.

By cultivating the habit of seeing the lighter side of drama, we ease the path toward self-love and acceptance. A humorous perspective lets us prioritize what truly matters, avoiding being overwhelmed by every minor incident. We learn to discern between genuine concerns and superficial frenzies, choosing to focus our emotional energies wisely.

So, the next time you find yourself embroiled in a dramatic episode over a spilled latte or a misinterpreted text message, pause and try visualizing it as if you're watching it unfold in a sitcom. You might find the absurdity tickling your funny bone rather than tightening your chest, helping you detach emotionally and preserve your peace of mind. Humor doesn't invalidate your feelings; it offers a refreshing lens through which we can visualize the impact of the drama on your life.

Summary And Reflections

As you close the pages of this chapter, remember that dodging unnecessary drama isn't about turning into an emotionless robot. It's more like becoming a drama ninja who knows when to gracefully duck and roll away from those chaotic situations that drain your emotional battery faster than a smartphone running with all the apps open. We've explored the whimsical world of the Drama Triangle and uncovered how we can unknowingly get cast in roles like victim or rescuer. Picture yourself armed with the knowledge that just because someone is playing out their soap opera scene, it doesn't mean you must also audition for a part.

But here's the ultimate twist: choosing to step off this dizzying carousel of melodrama frees up your time to star in your own story—a sitcom of sorts where the fun outweighs the turmoil. Think about adopting boundaries like a superhero cape, swishing around as you say "no" without guilt and swerving around chaos with a chuckle. By conserving your precious energy, you can focus on self-love and put your emotional reserves toward things that make your heart sing—or at least hum pleasantly. So rewrite the narrative, let laughter guide your way, and keep your emotional ninjas ready for action!

CHAPTER 5

TOOLS FOR SELF-EMPOWERMENT

Self-empowerment is about equipping yourself with the tools needed to embrace yourself and tackle life head-on. In a world where opinions fly faster than memes, it's easy to let external judgments shape our self-worth. But fear not! This chapter dives into practical strategies to boost self-esteem and nurture self-love, turning ordinary routines into empowering rituals. Imagine facing daily challenges with a sense of humor and resilience, like a stand-up comic confident in their routine, unshaken by hecklers. With these tools, you'll find that developing a solid sense of self isn't just about standing tall—it's also about laughing heartily.

This chapter explores the magic of daily affirmations—simple yet powerful statements that redirect your mind toward positivity and set a tone for your day. You'll learn how tailoring these affirmations to suit your personal goals can transform mundane moments into fuel for your inner superhero. Additionally, we'll delve into building resilience, seeing setbacks not as brick walls but as curvy detours on a scenic journey. We'll touch on the art of journaling as a therapeutic escape and a tool for reflection. Lastly, discover the joy of visualization techniques and mindful decluttering and how creating a supportive environment fortified by social connections can propel you toward empowerment. These tangible practices won't just help rewrite your narrative; they'll have you starring in your own feel-good story, alive with wit and wisdom.

Daily Affirmations

Imagine standing in front of your bathroom mirror, toothbrush in hand, when you suddenly decide to have a pep talk with yourself—out loud. Sure, it might feel odd at first, but what if I told you that these quirky little declarations, known as daily affirmations, could be your secret weapon against negative self-talk? Armed with positive language, affirmations can reshape your self-perception and strengthen healthier beliefs about yourself.

Perhaps you're wondering, "Why should I chat myself up every morning?" Well, here's the thing: positive language, like freshly brewed coffee, jolts your brain awake—trust me, science backs this up. According to various studies on behavioral interventions (Sherman & Cohen, 2006), affirming oneself helps counter psychological threats. So, when you proclaim, "I am capable," you're not just spouting feel-good fluff; you're actively challenging those nagging doubts that threaten your inner peace.

But let's not get carried away with generic mantras plastered all over Pinterest. For affirmations to hit home, they must be as personal as your fingerprint. Crafting personalized affirmations aligned with individual goals is critical. Imagine striving to become a marathon runner. Instead of a bland, "I am healthy," try something more potent like, "I am strong and getting stronger with every run." See the difference? Personalizing your affirmations ensures motivation doesn't fade faster than your phone's battery on the day you forgot to recharge it.

Creating effective affirmations isn't rocket science, but there's an art to it. Start by identifying areas where you'd like to see growth—maybe it's confidence or creativity. Then, transform these ambitions into present-tense statements that evoke emotion. Keep it realistic but inspiring. Your goal here is to set intentions that resonate deeply, offering a gentle push to keep chasing those dreams.

Of course, these affirmations aren't meant to be a one-time gig. Much like brushing your teeth, they require routine and consistency. Just as you wouldn't expect pearly whites without regular brushing, don't expect a positive mindset without habitual reaffirmation. Repetition fosters habit formation, leading to long-term behavioral changes. In other words, your affirmations are like mental reps at the gym, building resilience and reinforcing positivity over time.

Now, let's sprinkle some magic dust onto your affirmation practice. Enter visualization—a technique that can supercharge those spoken words. Visualization paired with affirmations deepens their impact by making future goals feel within reach. Picture this: as you recite, "I am confident and successful," you vividly imagine acing that presentation or smashing through your to-do list like a pro. Visualization transforms abstract concepts into tangible outcomes, boosting belief and determination to achieve them.

A nifty guideline for visualization? First, close your eyes and envision scenes relevant to your affirmations. Immerse yourself fully—how does it look, sound, and feel? Embrace the sights, sounds, and emotions associated with your success. Allow yourself to indulge in these sensory-rich experiences, embodying your future victories until they become second nature for your mind.

Think of affirmations as the breadcrumbs leading you toward personal development. But remember, progress isn't always linear. There will be days when negativity creeps back in, whispering its sinister tales. On such days, doubling down on your affirmations and visualization becomes even more essential. By consistently practicing these techniques, you'll cultivate a robust defense against adversity—like a knight in shining armor warding off dragons.

For those prone to memory lapses or laziness (hey, no judgment here!), jotting down your affirmations can help. Scribble them on sticky notes and scatter them around your house—your bathroom mirror, computer screen, fridge, you name it. It's all about keeping those positive vibes top-of-mind, effortlessly reminding you of your daily awesomeness.

So, the next time self-doubt starts creeping into your brain, remember the power in daily affirmations. They might not solve everything overnight or are a panacea for life's woes. However, by embracing the potential of positive language, crafting personalized affirmations, maintaining consistency, and indulging in visualization, you're well-equipped to rewrite the narrative of who you are and what you can accomplish.

Building Resilience

Have you ever watched a toddler stumble and fall, only to bounce back up with a giggle? This is resilience in its purest form—a delightful cocktail of humor and self-compassion. As adults, we often lose sight of this natural ability to shake off life's missteps with laughter. Instead of dodging failure like a migraine, what if we embraced our blunders as part of the human experience? Resilience isn't about never falling; it's about shrugging off the dust, chuckling at our mishaps, and striding forward gracefully.

Imagine a scenario: Walking to your favorite café when you trip on absolutely nothing, sending your phone skidding across the pavement. Do you curse the universe or laugh at your lack of coordination? Choosing the latter lightens your mood and strengthens your resilience muscle. Humor protects against the onslaught of external judgments, allowing us to maintain self-love despite minor setbacks.

One practical strategy for fostering resilience is journaling. It might seem old school, but putting pen to paper allows you to reclaim power over challenging experiences. Picture this—you pour your frustrations onto the page, transforming them from daunting mountains into manageable molehills. Examining these written reflections allows you to see patterns and possibilities for growth. It's less about crafting poetic prose and more about capturing authentic emotion, giving you a safe space to work through inner turmoil.

Let's talk about social connections now. They're like Wi-Fi signals for our souls—more robust and reliable than other networks. The people we surround ourselves with play significant roles in our emotional resilience. Engaging with supportive friends or family reduces that isolating feeling we get when life decides to throw a curveball. Remember, even superheroes need sidekicks! Leaning on your tribe during tough times makes your burdens lighter and reinforces that you are never alone in your struggles.

When life hands you lemons, most suggest making lemonade. But why stop there when you can turn those lemons into an entertaining anecdote? Reframing failures by finding humor in them paves the way for creative problem-solving. Take Thomas Edison, for example. When asked about his many failed attempts at inventing the lightbulb, he famously said he had discovered "10,000 ways that won't work." By infusing humor into our slip-ups, we become more flexible thinkers, able to approach problems with fresh perspectives and innovative solutions.

However, it's essential to remember that building resilience doesn't happen overnight. It requires practice and persistence. Here's where guidelines come into play:

1. Journaling: Set aside weekly time to journal your thoughts and feelings. There is no need for Shakespearean sonnets—raw and honest entries work best. Reflect on what you've written to identify any lessons or new understandings.

2. Nurturing Social Bonds: Actively reach out to those who lift your spirits and encourage open conversations about challenges. Plan regular check-ins to fortify these valuable connections.

3. Humor in Failure: Challenge yourself to find the quirky side of setbacks. This could mean sharing your embarrassing moments with friends (and laughing at theirs) or simply seeing the absurdity in everyday situations.

Creating A Positive Environment

Creating a space that nurtures self-empowerment and bolsters self-love is like cultivating a garden. The environment around us profoundly impacts how we feel about ourselves. One of the simplest yet most effective ways to start this journey is through designing our personal spaces. Imagine your home as a reflection of your mind. When cluttered, it sends signals of chaos and negativity, affecting your mood and self-esteem. On the flip side, decluttering symbolizes removing negativity from your life and creating room for positivity. It's akin to opening a window to let in a fresh breeze of optimism.

For instance, consider Marie Kondo's approach to tidying up. Her philosophy encourages individuals to keep only what sparks joy, transforming spaces into havens of tranquility. By adopting such practices, you're not just cleaning your room—you're sweeping away mental cobwebs that hinder your self-esteem. A tidy space can lead to a tidy mind, fostering an environment ripe for self-love and empowerment.

Beyond personal spaces, surrounding yourself with positive people is crucial. Building a community that brings laughter and support is like constructing a fortress around your well-being. Friends who lift you when you're down or share a laugh during tough times act as pillars of strength, reinforcing your empowerment. A study published in the Journal of Happiness Studies found that engaging with supportive social networks boosts happiness and resilience. By spending time with those who encourage rather than criticize, you cultivate a nourishing atmosphere for growth.

It's also essential to be mindful of the media we consume. In this digital age, we're bombarded with images and messages that can either build us up or break us down. Consuming media that uplifts and motivates fosters a more positive outlook on life. Steer clear of content that encourages unfavorable comparisons and instead seeks stories of triumph and perseverance. As noted by a participant in Vaingankar's study (2022), social media can provide encouragement and recognition, offering avenues for self-awareness and boosting self-esteem.

Guidelines for executing these ideas can be straightforward yet impactful. Start by designating a specific area in your home as a clutter-free zone, a sanctuary where only positive energy flows. Make it a habit to spend a few moments there each day, absorbing its peace and clarity. To build a community of positivity, focus on nurturing relationships with those who genuinely support your journey. This might mean reaching out to old friends or joining groups where laughter and support are the norms.

While mindfulness exercises typically urge focus and tranquility, don't underestimate the power of humor within this practice. Celebrate minor successes with a lighthearted spirit; perhaps have a joke jar to dip into, providing an instant pick-me-up after completing a daily task.

Incorporating these strategies creates an environment where self-love can flourish. In turn, this supportive setting encourages resilience against external judgments, promoting an unshakeable foundation of self-esteem. Remember, the key to self-empowerment lies within and in the surrounding walls and people. This harmonious alliance between our surroundings and mindset becomes the fuel that drives growth and transformation.

Social Connections & Media Consumption

Navigating the maze of life's social interactions and media choices can often feel like attempting a comedy skit in front of a stone-faced audience. But fear not, for these elements are the keys to unlocking self-love and resilience. At the heart of this lies an essential truth: who you let into your circle matters more than you think.

Imagine your social interactions as a garden. People who uplift you are the sunflowers – bright, encouraging, and always facing the light. These friends tell you when spinach is stuck in your teeth but also cheer the loudest when you finally get that promotion. They share jokes that make you snort and laugh even on your worst days and continuously offer words that lift your spirit sky-high. Surrounding yourself with such positive energy cultivates a nourishing environment where self-esteem can blossom. But beware of the weeds – those who bring negativity might look harmless at first but can quickly overrun your mental flowerbed, smothering any chance of growth.

Humor in relationships isn't just the cherry on top; it's the glue holding everything together during tough times. Picture this: you've had a day where nothing seemed to go right—unparalleled spilled coffee and forgotten passwords. Your friend comes with a classic dad joke or a meme that hits home, and suddenly, the world doesn't seem so grim. Sharing laughs is like emotional CPR; it revives the parts of us beaten down by the daily grind. Humor becomes a bridge over troubled waters, deepening connections and serving as an effective coping mechanism to navigate challenges that life throws our way, almost like giving us a sneak peek behind life's curtain, showing us it's not all doom and gloom.

Now, if only choosing your media consumption was as easy as scrolling through cat videos. In reality, what we watch, read, or listen to plays a pivotal role in shaping our sense of self. The next time you settle in for an episode of your favorite show or flip through a fashion magazine, ask yourself: does this content inspire me? If your media diet consists of comparison-inducing, highlight-reel content, it may be time for a swap. Insert a little dose of humor and motivation instead. Comedy specials, uplifting podcasts, and motivational books are all excellent tools for chiseling away the facade of negativity, helping foster a constructive narrative about your own identity by actively choosing media that makes you laugh and encourages you to dream bigger.

Creating a curated collection of amusing resources isn't just a nice-to-have; it's a powerhouse strategy for ongoing self-development. Think back to childhood treasure hunts; only now are the treasures books, shows, and playlists that never fail to put a smile on your face. Compile a list of comedians whose humor speaks to your soul or authors whose writings resonate with endless possibilities. Every time a storm cloud hovers above, dig into this treasure chest for sunshine. It's like having a loyal sidekick on your journey to self-betterment, making your sometimes arduous path more enjoyable and engaging.

Moreover, recent studies suggest that savoring joyful experiences enhances resilience by increasing positivity, which can help combat feelings of depression and anxiety spurred by social comparisons (Andrade et al., 2023). This technique involves focusing on the details of happy moments rather than dwelling on shortcomings, thus facilitating a shift in mindset. Parallelly, selecting humorous and inspiring media – content that gives pleasure and purpose – contributes significantly to psychological well-being by fostering positive emotions and strengthening one's ability to face adversity (K. et al., 2020).

Bringing It All Together

As we wrap up this chapter, it's clear that equipping ourselves with practical tools like daily affirmations and embracing resilience can be a game-changer in fostering self-love. We're building a robust personal toolkit by turning that bathroom mirror pep talks into personal powerhouses and laughing off life's little stumbles. Remember, these strategies aren't about reaching perfection overnight but paving the way for long-term change with humor and heart. Whether we're crafting quirky affirmations or chuckling over our imperfections, the goal is to nurture self-compassion while developing a stronger sense of self.

So, keep sprinkling your path with personalized affirmations and letting humor guide your journey through setbacks. With each affirmation, you're not just talking but reshaping how you see yourself. And with every giggle over a misstep, you're strengthening your resilience for life's inevitable bumps. By engaging with supportive friends and choosing media that uplifts you, you're setting the stage for a positive environment where self-love thrives. It's less about finding a magical solution and more about enjoying the ride—snorts and all—as you grow into your best version.

REVIEWPAGE

First, I would love to thank you for purchasing my book, and I hope you are enjoying the content. I know your time is valuable, but please scan this QR code, which will take you to my book review page. I would appreciate your review. Again, Thank You.

G.R. STINTZI

CHAPTER 6

REDEFINING VALIDATION

Redefining validation is much like discovering that the magician's hat was empty all along—an illusion of grandeur when, in reality, what we seek can be found inside us. We often pursue external affirmation like a treasure hunt where X marks someone else's opinion, yet this path leads to a desert of self-doubt rather than an oasis of contentment. It's time to shift the narrative and embark on a new adventure where the map directs us inward, pointing to the buried treasure within our mindset. Imagine turning the spotlight away from the crowd and onto your unique qualities; it's akin to realizing you're the star of your one-person show, bursting with potential for self-written acts of acceptance.

Embracing this internal journey means grasping the essential tools scattered throughout the chapter. It starts with comprehending the dynamics of validation as if we're cartographers charting the uncharted territories of our psyche. This exploration includes untangling those cultural ropes that tether us to superficial measures of success and reframing the funhouse mirrors reflecting distorted self-images. Acknowledging and celebrating these newfound insights brings forth an orchestra of self-approval playing your theme song while you stand center stage, free from the need for external applause. Discover how implementing positive self-talk or even solitary reflection becomes a stepping stone toward mastery over your sense of worth. The chapter ultimately delivers a guidebook on releasing the grip of societal expectations and making space for your authentic self to thrive without judgment. So get ready to redefine your inner GPS and navigate towards a destination of profound self-acceptance.

Understanding Validation Dynamics

Imagine life as an amusement park, with external validation as the main attraction. It's like hopping onto a roller coaster filled with dizzying highs and gut-wrenching lows. One moment, you're riding high, basking in the glory of others' praises, and the next, plummeting into self-doubt when approval wanes. This fickle ride can be exhausting and deceptive, often leaving us wondering why we embarked on it in the first place.

The journey for external validation is much like being strapped into a never-ending loop of anticipation and disappointment. We instinctively chase after others' nods of approval, believing that their acceptance will affirm our worth. But just like the roller coaster's temporary thrill, the satisfaction derived from outside approval is fleeting. It fails to provide the lasting sense of self-worth that comes from within. The challenge lies in stepping off this wild ride and grounding ourselves in self-acceptance.

In pursuit of validation, many of us find ourselves trapped in the endless people-pleasing cycle. Picture yourself juggling flaming swords while balancing on a tightrope, all to hear an applauding audience. Exhausting, right? People-pleasing thrives on the belief that our value is tied to how well we cater to others' expectations. It's a trait deeply rooted in low self-esteem (People-Pleasing: A Breakdown of the Bad Habit and How to Kick It | Thriveworks, 2022). By constantly seeking approval, we sacrifice our needs and boundaries, convinced that our worth depends on fulfilling others' desires.

However, the illusion of control is precisely that—an illusion. While we aim to keep everyone around us happy like a dedicated circus performer, the reality is harsh. Our self-worth becomes entangled in a web of others' perceptions, draining energy that could otherwise nurture self-growth and acceptance. The escape from this pattern begins by understanding its roots, acknowledging that sometimes this behavior may even stem from past traumas, where pleasing others was a means to garner safety or attention. Realizing this, we can start untangling those threads and redirect our focus toward self-compassion.

Another layer adds complexity to this issue: cultural influences. Imagine stepping into a funhouse filled with mirrors, each reflection warping our perception of worth. Cultural norms, societal expectations, and the clamor of 'likes' and 'shares' shape these distorted reflections. Society broadcasts superficial measures of success, urging us to measure ourselves against unrealistic standards. This barrage of external cues contributes to the roller coaster of highs and lows as we either match up to the predefined image of worth or fall short.

Cultural impacts on people-pleasing are significant (<i>Physicians Can Easily Get Trapped in the Need for External Validation.</i>, 2021). Many societies emphasize politeness and conformity, pushing individuals to seek validation through adherence to communal norms. These cultural scripts dictate behavior, whispering that deviation equates to unworthiness. Yet, by recognizing these influences, we begin to dismantle the superficial markers assigned to us, freeing ourselves to define our measure of value beyond cultural confines.

Reflecting on personal experiences offers insights into our past validation moments. Think of it as sorting through postcards from your life's journey. Some are vivid reminders of genuine connections, while others fade quickly, leaving nothing but a trace of what once was. By examining these memories, we can discern between the transient and the significant aspects of our interactions.

This reflection unveils patterns, helping to identify instances where validation was driven more by the expectations of others rather than our intrinsic values. By revisiting these scenarios, we gain clarity on what genuinely uplifted us versus what was merely riding the coattails of external approval. More importantly, this practice empowers us to forge a deeper connection with our true selves, independent of the world's judgmental gaze.

Ultimately, breaking free from the need for constant external validation involves recognizing that self-worth isn't a hallmark bestowed by others. Instead, it's cultivated through embracing our uniqueness, setting healthy boundaries, and nurturing relationships that appreciate our authentic selves. Imagine replacing the roller coaster ride with a peaceful stroll through a garden you've tended with love and care; each plant represents your unwavering self-worth.

Cultivating Self-Approval

Have you ever sat and listened to that little voice in your head? You know the one—it criticizes your choice of breakfast cereals and questions your life choices. Developing a positive inner dialogue is like transforming that voice from a grumpy critic into a supportive friend who always has your back. Rather than berating yourself for missing that morning run, imagine this new voice celebrating the simple fact that you've learned to press snooze at the perfect moment. This shift doesn't happen overnight, but consistently catching negative thoughts and flipping them into positives can work wonders for your self-esteem.

Establishing little rituals can help kickstart this conversation with yourself. Allow me to introduce the daily affirmation habit. It's like breakfast for your brain! Every morning, toss in a handful of "I am capable" and "I embrace growth" and watch your day blossom. Over time, you'll discover that consistent affirmations can become second nature, gradually replacing those pesky self-doubts. After all, why rely on others to tell us how fabulous we are when we can say it to ourselves?

And speaking of celebrating, let's talk about throwing confetti over personal achievements—big and small. Forget waiting for someone else to recognize your accomplishments; it's time to be your hype person. Have you finished a project? Fabulous! Manage to water your plants before they stage a sit-down? Incredible! Celebrating these moments reinforces your sense of worth, no matter how seemingly minor. The key here is consistency; list what went well each day, no matter how tiny. Relish the satisfaction of being able to tick off your triumphs. You deserve every pat on the back!

As you navigate adulthood, solitude might seem like an old friend or a terrifying specter. Yet, embracing time alone can feel like revamping your living room—at first, daunting but ultimately rewarding. Spending time alone provides opportunities for reflection. It's where you face the chaos in your mind, learning that enjoying your company is okay. Solitude allows space for honest introspection without the noise of external opinion, leading to genuine self-acceptance.

Picture this: instead of seeking validation from that one friend who judges everything from your hairstyle to your hobby choices, you find contentment in a quiet afternoon with a book or flying your new kite on the beach. (Yes, I live next to a beach!) Reflect on what makes you chuckle, ponder, or even tear up. Not every moment needs to be populated with likes and comments. Maybe spend an evening asking yourself, "What do I want?" minus input from social media polls.

Let's discuss practicing gratitude for oneself. We love to write gratitude lists for sunsets and dogs, but what about appreciating our resilience and quirks? Shifting focus from external to internal satisfaction means taking a moment to thank yourself for being resilient after a challenging week or patient during life's little annoyances. You're not just surviving; you're thriving, even if some days thrive looks suspiciously like a couch potato.

Start a self-gratitude journal—jot down three things you appreciate about yourself daily. Whether it's your killer knack for whipping up dinner from leftovers or your ability to empathize with a friend, these acknowledgments pile up, forming a solid foundation of self-worth.

So, how do you begin this journey? Create a cozy corner for contemplation. Start with mindful breathing exercises that calm the relentless pace of life. As you become more attuned to your needs without external validation, you'll notice that your self-approval blooms naturally. The need for others to see and validate your worth diminishes slowly.

Incorporating humorous self-talk can transform your relationship with yourself. Humor lightens the load, allowing you to laugh at mishaps rather than dwell in criticism. Remember, laughter is a universal language; speak it fluently in your self-dialogue. Imagine your inner critic as a stand-up comedian with punchlines like, "My memory is so bad that I have to write down everything I want to forget." Ah, you've just added a splash of creativity to the morning!"

Letting Go Of Others' Expectations

In a world that often measures success by the approval of others, finding your voice can feel like navigating a maze. Yet, embracing authenticity allows you to break free from this labyrinth, leading to personal freedom. Imagine no longer shaping your actions based on perceived judgment but living in a way that honors your true self. Take Peter, for example, who decided to leave his corporate job to pursue a career in culinary arts. At first, people questioned his decision, viewing it as a risky departure from societal norms. However, Peter found joy and a renewed purpose by embracing his passion. Living authentically doesn't just mean doing what you love; it's about aligning every aspect of your life with your internal values, creating coherence between who you are inside and how you present yourself to the world.

Setting personal boundaries is crucial in this journey toward authenticity. Boundaries act as a protective shield, allowing you to prioritize your needs without guilt or fear of judgment. Consider them as invisible lines that define your comfort zone. They help you filter out negativity and maintain your mental health by ensuring that you engage in activities and relationships that nurture rather than drain you. To illustrate, Sarah learned to say no to weekend work meetings, a step that allowed her to dedicate time to her family and personal growth. By setting clear boundaries, she protected her energy and redefined what success meant for her. Establishing such parameters isn't just empowering; it's an essential guideline for anyone seeking genuine self-expression.

Equally important is surrounding yourself with encouraging people who celebrate your uniqueness. Think of these individuals as your tribe, those who affirm your worth even when you doubt yourself. Having a supportive network promotes authenticity because it permits you to shed pretenses and be vulnerable without fear of rejection. In a company where acceptance is unconditional, discarding the mask of conformity becomes easier. For instance, attending a creative writing group where members openly share their stories can bolster confidence and reinforce the belief that being different is okay. Cultivating these relationships requires discernment, but investing in connections that allow you to be your genuine self is invaluable.

Developing a humorous outlook on judgments is another powerful tool. Learning to laugh at criticism diminishes its power and highlights its absurdity. Remember that not everyone will understand your path, and that's perfectly fine. Humor offers a fresh perspective on criticisms that might otherwise dwarf your spirit. Suppose someone mocks your choice to start over in midlife; seeing the comedy in their narrow-mindedness can remind you that their opinion holds no weight in your quest for authenticity. Humor acts as a buffer, softening the sting of judgment and enabling you to navigate social critiques gracefully. This approach doesn't negate the value of constructive feedback but instead differentiates valuable insights from baseless censure.

Stripping away the layers of expectation to reveal your authentic self is a courageous act that empowers you to live fully and freely. Embracing authenticity means understanding that you are not beholden to the judgments of others, nor do you need to justify your choices to fit into predetermined molds. By setting personal boundaries, you carve out space for self-care and assert your right to live according to your values. Surrounding yourself with like-minded individuals further solidifies your resolve, creating a community that nurtures rather than suppresses your individuality. When faced with naysayers, adopting a humorous outlook can transform criticisms into lessons in resilience.

Finding Joy In Authentic Living

In a world obsessed with fitting in, the quest for external validation often overshadows the joy of living authentically. Yet, embracing your individuality can lead to profound personal satisfaction and happiness. So, let's dive into how ditching societal norms in favor of authenticity could be the most fun you've had in ages.

First up is individuality. Picture this: you, as a unique snowflake—or maybe a quirky tree amidst a forest—embracing your distinct shape rather than blending into the arboreal scenery.

Research suggests that a sense of uniqueness isn't just a self-indulgent navel-gazing act; it's deeply associated with authentic living and happiness (Koydemir et al., 2018). You're setting yourself toward more profound satisfaction when you recognize what makes you. Think of it as discovering the hidden superpower within your quirks and eccentricities—like realizing you've always been fluent in sarcasm or that your love of obscure indie films is a staple conversational piece. Embracing individuality isn't just freeing; it's exhilarating.

Now, onto the playground of passions and interests. Authentic living allows you to dive headfirst into things you genuinely care about. Forget about society's rigid checklist of acceptable hobbies. You have the license to explore anything, whether synchronized swimming or an encyclopedic knowledge of wild mushrooms. The key is minimizing that mismatch between conscious awareness and experience (Patrick, 2021). Doing what you love simply because you love it invites genuine happiness into your life. Imagine spending Saturday mornings at the farmer's market instead of conforming to brunch clichés and or pursuing that long-forgotten dream of learning to scuba dive. Freedom in passion breeds happiness and stories worth retelling—stories where you find joy in every odd place you dare venture.

But wait! What's authenticity if not expressed through relationships? Forming connections based on mutual appreciation is like finding a partner who enjoys discussing whether aliens exist. These connections aren't about bowing to social clicks and glamour; they're built on sincerity and respect. Relationships rooted in authenticity encourage self-expression and empower you to live unapologetically. As your circle grows with those who appreciate your uniqueness, you'll feel supported in replacing scripted pleasantries for heartfelt conversations. It's like hosting a dinner party where everyone shows up as they indeed are, and no one cares if someone forgot to bring a salad—it's all about being together, as real as it gets.

Lastly, viewing life through an authentic lens enhances everyday experiences. It's like wearing glasses after years of living in a blurry world. Suddenly, there's beauty in the mundane. Daily routines become opportunities to relish life's little quirks. A commute becomes a chance to belt out your favorite '90s tunes, or the evening walk becomes an exploration of neighborhood mysteries. Through authenticity, ordinary days transform, revealing snippets of humor and joy hiding in plain sight. It's almost as if you're a detective in a comedy mystery of life—piecing together smiles from bits of chaos around you.

Embracing authenticity might seem daunting in a world bent on pigeonholing people into boxes labeled by trends and expectations. However, when you commit to living authentically— embracing individuality, pursuing true passions, cultivating sincere relationships, and cherishing simple moments—you lay the groundwork for a fulfilling life. Authentic living encourages saying "no" to superficial judgments and "yes" to delighting in your skin. It's a wild, colorful ride filled with detours and unexpected discoveries—a journey where the destination is happiness.

Summary And Reflections

So, here we are, bravely stepping off the roller coaster of external validation and waving goodbye to that dizzying ride. We've been on a whirlwind tour through a theme park of societal expectations, cultural influences, people-pleasing antics, and the bright lights of social media approval. We've explored how chasing after others' acceptance is like trying to catch smoke with your bare hands— impossible and ultimately exhausting. Instead of riding that coaster endlessly, we're now focused on grounding ourselves in self-acceptance, nurturing relationships that bring out our true selves, and building a foundation of self-worth from within.

As the chapter draws to a close, it's all about finding joy in living authentically, embracing our quirks, and becoming our favorite hype person. The journey to ditching other people's opinions might have awkward stumbles or comedic slip-ups, but those moments make it worthwhile. By setting personal boundaries, engaging in genuine connections, and adding a dash of humor to our inner dialogue, we're forging a path to fulfillment that's uniquely ours. So, let's leave behind the tick-tick of the roller coaster ascent and enjoy a peaceful walk through a garden of self-worth, where our compass guides every step.

CHAPTER 7

EMBRACE THE UNIQUENESS

Embracing your uniqueness is like discovering a hidden treasure that you never knew you possessed. It's the kind of revelation that can make even the dullest day feel like an adventure waiting to happen. Imagine waking up one morning and realizing that those little quirks you often shrugged off are your secret tools for navigating life's winding paths. Maybe you've always been that person who collects random trivia, or perhaps you have a laugh that turns heads from miles away. These seemingly trivial things are not just part of who you are; they make you undeniably unique in a world that often tries to fit everyone into a predefined mold.

In this chapter, we're going to take a journey through the colorful landscape of individuality. We'll delve into the idea that self-acceptance is the first step toward recognizing your unique traits as superpowers rather than oddities. There will be discussions on identifying these personal gems and how they can shape your life path in ways you'd never imagined. From organizing spice racks with precision to finding joy in niche interests like dinosaur facts, we'll explore how these facets contribute to a fulfilling life. More importantly, you'll learn to document and celebrate these traits, turning them into daily reminders of your distinctiveness. Along the way, we'll offer tips on creating environments that encourage authenticity and connections. This chapter is about finding the confidence to parade through life just as you are, complete with puns, dance moves, and all the joyful eccentricities you bring to the table.

Identifying Unique Traits

Recognizing and appreciating our unique qualities can be fresh air in a world where we're constantly encouraged to blend in. Have you ever considered that your quirks — those seemingly odd traits you've never paid much attention to — are your superpowers? Well, it's time to harness them.

Let's start with the journey of knowing thyself. We're talking about digging deep to identify personality traits and peculiarities that define us. Here's a little secret: self-acceptance is like having an internal pep rally, cheering you on as you parade through life. For example, maybe you love organizing everything from spice racks to sock drawers. While others might roll their eyes, this trait could make you the go-to person for project management or event planning, showcasing your meticulous nature and thoughtfulness.

Speaking of uniqueness, remember everyone has something special — even if it seems tiny or insignificant. Think back to school days: there was always one kid who could draw detailed superheroes or another who knew every spec of a "70 Chevelle Malibu. Those once 'trivial' skills can become the foundation for a fulfilling career or hobby in adulthood. Celebrate these facets of yourself! You're not just ordinary; you're like a mosaic of distinctive pieces, each adding value to the whole picture.

Here's a fun idea: keep a 'unique traits' journal to dig into what makes you, well, you! Jotting down things you love about yourself — that infectious laugh, the knack for solving crossword puzzles in record time, or your ability to whip up a gourmet meal from leftovers — can be a confidence booster whenever you're feeling blah. Imagine flipping through this journal during a rainy day and instantly being reminded of the beautiful things that make you... you. This exercise is an ongoing celebration of your individuality, perfect for recognizing personal growth.

There's something unapologetically memorable about quirky traits often deemed flaws by societal standards. Take, for instance, an unconventional sense of humor — perhaps you find puns irresistible while others groan. This flair for the unexpected can turn you into someone people remember long after a party is over. Own it and watch how these quirks transform interactions and leave lasting impressions.

One famous example is Albert Einstein. Renowned for his messy hair and unconventional thinking, he changed the course of science. His distinctiveness wasn't just in his ideas but in embracing who he was and his quirks. Your quirks may not result in groundbreaking theories (or who knows, maybe they will), but they certainly make you irreplaceable in your social circle, workplace, or home.

It's easy to get caught up in societal pressures to conform, but think of conformity as a monochrome painting — pleasant yet lacking spark. Adding your unique elements turns life vibrant and full of texture. So, next time you're tempted to squash down that silly dance move that only you know, remember: it's part of your delightfully complex tapestry.

And if you ever feel bogged down by mainstream expectations, look at some of the world's greatest inventors, artists, and leaders. Unlike the text copied from a manual, they broke molds to forge their paths — paths that were far from ordinary. Their success lay in proudly flaunting their uniqueness.

So, let's infuse some humor into the narrative of life's seriousness. Let your freak flags fly high! We allow others to do the same when we embrace our true selves, complete with clumsy moments and eccentric habits. This becomes a domino effect of authenticity and genuine connections, building communities that thrive on diversity rather than uniformity.

Owning Your Differences

In the grand tapestry of humanity, our unique threads add vibrancy and depth. Imagine life without diversity—it'd be like a movie where every character is the same: predictable and, frankly, a bit dull. Embracing what makes us different isn't just a personal victory; it's a societal necessity. It's the quirks, the unexpected perspectives, and yes, even the oddities that spark creativity and innovation, driving progress in a world craving originality.

Consider the creators of our favorite gadgets or the writers of stories that transport us to other worlds. They're not following some universal formula. They draw from their unique wells of experience. Why? Because personal differences fuel the kind of thinking that breaks molds and forges new paths. We have virtual reality games, self-driving cars, and a myriad of other wonders borne from the minds of those who dared to be different. Embrace the weirdness—it might lead to the next big thing: Flying cars, yes! They are working on the prototypes now.

But how do you showcase these unique perspectives? It starts with finding your voice and spotlighting your ideas in the noisy room of societal expectations. Communicating effectively isn't about dominating the conversation; it's about articulating your thoughts confidently and clearly. Think of ways to express yourself that resonate with others—through art, writing, speeches, or everyday interactions.

Imagine you're interested in growing rare succulents—quirky, right? Share your passion by engaging with enthusiasts online or starting a blog. Not only does this let your individuality shine, but it also encourages others to appreciate niches that make them stand out. Speaking up doesn't mean shouting; it's about choosing the right words, audience, and time to share your uniqueness with the world.

Locating your tribe can further bolster your sense of self-worth. In a sea of sameness, there are pockets of people who cherish diversity, eagerly welcoming those willing to break the mold. Social media and community groups abound with individuals searching for connections based on shared interests or characteristics. Engage with these communities—they're havens where individuality flourishes and collective creativity blossoms.

For instance, perhaps you've always felt like a square peg in a round hole, but then you discover a local theater group that thrives on eccentricity. Through this group, you realize you're not alone. You're inspired by fellow actors who embrace their theatrical quirks, turning them into strengths on stage. These connections provide a sense of belonging while reinforcing the value of standing apart from the crowd.

History is peppered with tales of people whose peculiarities paved the road to greatness. Many have successfully leveraged their differences from Einstein's thought experiments during solitary walks to Lady Gaga's avant-garde performances. Their stories serve as lighthouses, guiding us to see that nonconformity often leads to innovation and personal fulfillment. (WRITER, 2024)

Take the story of Emily Dickinson—a reclusive poet whose works were discovered posthumously and went on to shape modern poetry. " A word is dead when it is said, some say. I say it just begins to live that day." Her unconventional lifestyle allowed her to observe the world with fresh eyes, creating a legacy celebrated long after she left this earth. Such narratives remind us that rather than fitting in, tapping into our singular traits can carve pathways to success.

Here's something wonderfully counterintuitive: embracing your oddities invites others to do the same. Celebrating your true self allows those around you to shrug off societal pressures and show their authentic selves. Picture a domino effect of authenticity that starts with you. Each person you inspire becomes another beacon of uniqueness in a world full of clones.

When we see someone boldly express themselves, it resonates deeply. Maybe you've noticed this when observing a coworker who isn't afraid to wear vibrant outfits that reflect their personality. Their confidence is contagious, encouraging others in the workplace to dress more freely and unapologetically express themselves. This ripple effect fosters a more inclusive environment and enhances overall morale and creativity within the team.

Life is far too short to spend mimicking others at the expense of what makes you, well, you. Whether it's an affinity for painting cat portraits or an obsession with medieval history, take pride in your interests. The world doesn't need more copies; it needs originals, paving the way for a society rich in diversity and innovation.

Breaking Away From Conformity

The pressure to conform to societal expectations can be overwhelming in a world that sometimes operates on a "one-size-fits-all" mentality. But have you ever stopped to think about whose standards you're trying to meet? Society often dictates how we should look, behave, and even dream. Yet, the harm of unthinkingly following these norms is frequently overlooked. When we're so focused on fitting in, we might lose sight of who we are.

Critically examining societal expectations begins with asking ourselves tough questions: Why do I feel compelled to behave or present myself in a certain way? Who set these standards, and do they serve my happiness? When you analyze these societal pressures, it becomes clear that many are arbitrary. They're rooted in traditions or outdated beliefs that don't necessarily align with our personal values or modern realities. Consider, for example, the old notion that success is synonymous with a high-paying job and a shiny car. For many, happiness might instead lie in creative pursuits or enriching life experiences that defy conventional measures of success.

Exploring harmless nonconformity can be an empowering experience. Nonconformity doesn't mean rebelling for rebellion; instead, it's about making choices that reflect your true self, even if those choices are at odds with mainstream expectations. Maybe for you, this means mixing and matching clothes in ways that express your unique style, regardless of what's on the fashion page. Or perhaps it involves pursuing a career path that prioritizes passion over prestige. Whatever form it takes, embracing your differences allows you to express self-acceptance openly and honestly.

There's a profound strength in the stories of people who've broken away from the mold and redefined what it means to live authentically. Take J.K. Rowling, for instance, who faced numerous rejections before finding success with Harry Potter. Her story illustrates the power of persistence and staying true to one's vision despite external pressures. Similarly, Steve Jobs' commitment to innovative technology laid the groundwork for products that revolutionized industries. These individuals didn't let societal norms dictate their paths. Instead, they embraced their uniqueness, which ultimately led to groundbreaking achievements.

Setting personal standards grounded in happiness and self-love can act as a guiding light through life's myriad challenges. It may take time and reflection, but understanding what makes you genuinely happy is invaluable. Think about what activities make you lose track of time or fill you with joy. Let these pursuits guide your decisions rather than constantly seeking validation from others. When your actions stem from a place of self-love and contentment, you're less likely to feel the need to compare yourself to others and more likely to find satisfaction in your journey.

Feedback and reflection can play crucial roles in developing self-awareness. Sometimes, we're too close to our lives to see things. Here's where friends come in handy. We gain insights that might otherwise escape us by tapping into their perspectives. Have a candid conversation with your closest confidants. Ask them what they admire about you. Their responses might surprise you and offer a fresh lens through which to view yourself. This exercise can be incredibly beneficial in combating negative self-talk and building a stronger sense of self-worth.

As we journey through life, it's essential to remember that there's no universal blueprint for happiness or success. Embracing your authentic self involves defining personal standards infused with joy rather than dictated by fear of judgment. Seek group settings where unique traits are celebrated collectively. Whether through a themed social gathering or a collaborative project, sharing what makes each person unique can foster an environment of mutual support and admiration.

Creating A Personal "Superpower" List

Celebrating your unique traits is like finding a hidden superpower in a world where everyone seems fixated on fitting into certain molds. It's time to invite some fun into the mix with an exercise that transforms self-discovery from daunting to delightful: creating your "Superpower" list.

Imagine this: You sit down with a notepad, a favorite beverage, and maybe even a silly hat because why not? Your mission? To jot down all those qualities, skills, and quirks that make you unabashedly you. Perhaps you're the person who can keep a plant alive longer than anyone else—others may call it a green thumb, but we know it's plant-whisperer-level stuff. Or maybe you have an uncanny ability to remind everyone of their appointments without breaking a sweat. As you write, let each word be a little badge of honor contributing to a positive self-image, spotlighting your individuality.

Here's the kicker: These unique traits aren't just for show. Think of them as tools in your utility belt, ready to boost you personally and professionally. Channeling these 'superpowers' can add a dash of magic to everyday situations. For example, if your superpower is terrific storytelling, imagine how that could elevate your presentations at work, making them memorable and engaging. Playing to your strengths makes you likely feel more engaged, productive, and genuinely fulfilled (Pascoe, 2023).

But let's not stop there. Just like any superhero's powers evolve, so should your list. Life has a way of throwing new experiences, challenges, and opportunities our way; hence, updating your list isn't just encouraged; it's essential. Each new chapter of your life might unearth fresh talents or enhance existing ones. Maybe today, you're a master pasta chef, and next year, you'll discover your flair for painting landscapes. Keep your list dynamic and reflective of your growth journey.

And here's an exciting twist—why not rope in some trusty sidekicks, otherwise known as friends? After all, they often see qualities in you that you might overlook. Ask them what they think your superpowers are, and use this feedback as fuel to expand your self-awareness. This can also be a powerful antidote to negative self-talk, helping you refocus on the attributes that truly define you.

Now, let's dive a bit deeper. These unique qualities aren't confined to hobbies or weekend projects. They hold the potential to transform your career and relationships. When you're conscious of your strengths, choices become more apparent. You start investing time in pursuits that utilize your inherent talents, leading to greater satisfaction and perhaps even new avenues for professional advancement (Pascoe, 2023).

For instance, consider empathy—a quality that's often underestimated. In a world striving for innovation, those who excel at understanding others pave the way for more effective teamwork and leadership. Similarly, creativity doesn't merely belong to artists and writers; it drives problem-solving across industries. Recognizing such traits in yourself paves the way for carving out niches where you can shine most brightly.

As you bask in the glow of your awesomeness, remember that your journey of self-discovery isn't meant to be solitary or static. The real magic happens when you merge introspection with insights from those you trust. By seeking out and appreciating constructive feedback, you cultivate a holistic view of yourself, reinforcing the narrative of self-worth and resilience.

So, take a moment to celebrate your superpowers—write them down, revisit them often, and wear them with pride. Let your list remind you of your irreplaceable place in this vibrant world. These unique traits, skills, and qualities set you apart and allow you to leave your fingerprint on every great adventure that comes your way.

Bringing It All Together

In this chapter, we've taken a colorful dive into the vibrant ocean of individuality, exploring how embracing our quirks can add a splash of color to the sometimes monochrome canvas of life. We've chatted about recognizing those little traits that we often tuck away and realizing their potential as superpowers. From organizing spice racks with military precision to remembering obscure dinosaur facts, these unique qualities make you remarkable. As readers, you've armed yourselves with the tools to flip through your own 'unique traits' journal whenever life tries to convince you otherwise.

As you step away from societal expectations and let your authentic self take center stage, remember that life is too short to dance to someone else's beat when you have your funky rhythm waiting to groove. Celebrate the quirks, the oddities, and the things that make you stand out. And don't just keep them to yourself— share them with the world! Whether through that blog about rare succulents or the unexpected flash mob at the office, your individuality becomes a beacon for others to shine. So go ahead, wave that freak flag high, and watch as the dominoes of authenticity create a community that thrives on diversity, shunning conformity in favor of genuine connections.

CHAPTER 8

NAVIGATING SOCIAL MEDIA MYTHS

Today's social media is like attempting to walk a tightrope in the middle of a circus, where the crowd's roar is just the din of likes and comments. You step gingerly forward, eyes on the high wire of perfect selfies, exotic vacations, and endless brunch spreads that dazzle the virtual spectators below. The thrill lies not just in the balancing act itself but in the understanding—or somewhat, misunderstanding—what it means to be under the spotlight. Capturing only the best angles might seem like an art form, but it's also where myths begin to spin their tales. Social media myths have more twists and turns than a Hollywood plotline, convincing us that everyone else lives in a perpetual state of glamour. Before you can say "Photoshop," you're swept away by this digital fantasy land where every day is sunny and unblemished.

In this chapter, we'll embark on an insightful adventure through these online myths that paint a surreal canvas of influence over self-worth. We'll peek behind the filtered curtain to understand how influencers craft the illusion of perfection and explore the trail they leave, laden with inspiration and unrealistic ideals. Discover tools for cultivating authenticity amid the crafted chaos and offering new insight through which to view your own life. From understanding the fine line between motivation and envy, each click and swipe becomes a chance to rewrite your narrative with honesty and, perhaps, a little bit of digital detoxing.

Behind-The-Scenes Reality

In today's digital age, social media has become a window through which we present our lives to the world. But let's be honest—it's more like a stained-glass window than a plain one. The colors, patterns, and highlights you see are carefully selected pieces that aim to dazzle and impress. Welcome to the Highlight Reel Effect, a concept that underscores how social media often showcases only the best moments of our lives. This carefully curated content creates an illusion that everyone else's life is a constant party, where the fun never stops, and everything is picture-perfect.

But remember, behind every smiling selfie on a fabulous vacation or a perfectly staged dinner photo lies a reality far less glamorous. We're all guilty of being directors of our highlight reels, capturing those fleeting moments that reflect the life we want others to believe we have. When scrolling through these polished snapshots, it's easy to fall into the trap of unrealistic expectations, assuming that others' lives are always better or happier than our own. It's not surprising, then, as some studies suggest that constant exposure to these curated displays can lead to feelings of inadequacy and depression (Murray, 2019).

Another layer to this digital mirage is the wonders of Photoshop, edits, and filters. These tools can turn ordinary images into seemingly magical visuals, drastically altering appearances and creating fantastical versions of reality. Impossibly smooth skin, endless legs, and ethereal backdrops become everyday occurrences in our feeds. Yet, beneath these edited layers is an unfiltered truth: these manipulated images contribute to a distorted sense of beauty and success. They set standards that are not just difficult but often impossible to achieve. It's like living in a perpetual fantasy land where everyone looks like they've just stepped off a fashion runway, leading us to forget that blemishes, wrinkles, and bad hair days are part of what makes us human. The Kardashians, need I say more!

The life of influencers—social media celebrities—is another puzzle piece in our journey through the online maze. Their vibrant posts often depict a lifestyle filled with exotic travel, luxurious brands, and perfect relationships, making it seem like they've cracked the code to a dream existence. However, these portrayals can be anything but authentic. Behind the scenes, influencers face their struggles, pressures, and mundane realities. The glamorized images we consume can lead us to chase ideals that may not only be unattainable but also inauthentic. As much as influencers might inspire us, we must remind ourselves that their posts could reflect strategic brand partnerships rather than personal fulfillment.

While navigating this landscape of manufactured perfection, finding ways to engage with social media authentically becomes crucial. Here comes the guiding light: cultivating a mindful approach to how and what we consume online is essential for maintaining a healthy relationship with social media. Begin by filtering your social media input with intention. Follow creators who offer diverse perspectives and share both successes and struggles honestly. You deconstruct the façade of flawlessness and invite authenticity into your virtual sphere.

Engaging in regular social media detoxes can also help ground us in reality, allowing us to disconnect from the constant barrage of counterfeit content. Taking breaks from screens gives us space to reconnect with our true selves and those around us without the filter of technology. Such practices encourage self-reflection and a deeper understanding of the influence that social media has on our emotions and self-perception. Instead of consuming content passively, engage actively, questioning the presented narratives and how they align with your values and truth. By doing so, you're not just freeing yourself from unrealistic standards but embracing the beautifully imperfect reality of life beyond the screen.

Filters Vs. Authenticity

Have you ever taken a casual scroll through your social media feed and wondered if everyone else lives in an alternate universe? You know, the one where every picture looks like it belongs on a magazine cover? Welcome to the world of altered depictions— where reality meets a touch of magic, courtesy of digital filters. It's a realm we all frequent yet seldom speak of with honesty.

This phenomenon, known as 'The Filter Phenomenon,' has quietly reshaped our perceptions of reality and personal expectations. With just a swipe or a tap, you can transform what was once an ordinary snapshot into a post worthy of envy. Now, who wouldn't want to look Insta-glamorous at all times? Yet, with great power comes great responsibility. The constant use of filters beautifies images and warps our understanding of what's real. Behind the façade of flawless skin and perfect lighting lies a simple truth—these modifications create a distorted standard that no one can perpetually uphold (MORESCHI, 2022).

Our digital landscapes are bustling with pressure to appear 'perfect,' fueling an anxiety epidemic. It starts innocuously. That little voice in your head whispers, "Why does no one 'like' my unedited posts?" Suddenly, you're spiraling down a rabbit hole of self-doubt. Social pressures amplify this emotional tumult, setting up high bars and inviting us to measure ourselves against meticulously curated versions of others. And that's when things start to get tricky. We find ourselves striving for impossible standards—an inherently futile chase because those ideals are steeped in illusion, not reality.

Now, let's take a minute to laugh at ourselves here. We've all been guilty of editing a pimple from a selfie or enhancing our breakfast to look more vibrant than a rainbow, haven't we? No harm, no foul there—as long as it doesn't become the norm. If your digital presence feels more like a masquerade than a mirror, it might be time to pause and ponder. The essence of authentic self-expression lies in balancing the filtered and the unfiltered, the curated and the candid.

And speaking of candid moments, let's talk about embracing authentic communication and sharing those genuine, imperfect snippets of life. Oh, they're gold! They invite real connections. Think about it. When was the last time you saw an unfiltered photo and thought, "Wow, now that's relatable"? Probably not too long ago! It's ironic how showing vulnerability and rawness can draw people closer together in this heavily edited world. That silly snap with bedhead, morning coffee, or the slightly embarrassing dance video can resonate far more deeply than any posed, polished shot. So next time, try posting something raw—it might be the most refreshing thing you've done online in ages!

Venturing back into reality for a moment, let's not sugarcoat the consequences of these comparisons. The emotional toll from consistently measuring oneself against these perfected images is palpable and concerns mental health experts (Bounds, 2024). Persistent exposure to idealized images can trigger feelings of inadequacy or lower self-esteem, particularly among young adults and teens who are still shaping their identities. According to studies, such ongoing comparisons have been linked to increased occurrences of anxiety and depression. It's like being stuck in a never-ending beauty pageant where the judges' opinions are the only ones that matter—and spoiler alert: they're always looking for perfection.

Breaking this cycle requires a shift towards valuing authenticity over illusions. We can alleviate some internal pressures by cultivating genuine interactions rather than executing flawless performances. Moreover, this means recognizing that while filters can enhance beauty and entertain, they should not dictate the narrative of self-worth or the perception of reality. It's about understanding their place—a tool for expression, not a measure of value.

Imagine substituting judgment with acceptance, both online and offline. Allow yourself to embrace the beautifully imperfect human experience. Give space for flaws and quirks in your digital footprints. It's okay if every day isn't Instagram-worthy; life doesn't come pre-packaged in perfect light and angles. Celebrate the messiness and color outside the lines once in a while.

It's liberating to step back from the polished parade parading past your feeds and kindly remind yourself that you are more than just pixels on a screen. Your worth isn't tethered to your social media persona but derives from your actions, experiences, and how you engage with the world around you—in all its beautiful chaos.

Impact Of Online Opinions

In today's digital age, social media's impact on personal self-image is undeniable. Whether it's likes, comments, or retweets, engagement numbers often become an unofficial measure of self-worth. Picture this: you proudly post a vacation snapshot on Instagram, but as minutes tick by with minimal likes, doubt creeps in—did I choose the wrong filter? Was my pose awkward?

This constant craving for validation through likes and shares can create a skewed perception of self-worth. Unlike the tangible compliments or constructive feedback we receive face-to-face, social media interactions are fleeting and can leave one feeling inadequate without immediate approval. A study cited by Acosta (Smith, 2023) suggests that such pressure to maintain a likable online persona leads individuals toward unhealthy behaviors like excessive self-promotion and attention-seeking.

Moreover, social media platforms double as arenas for toxic comments and harassment. Hidden behind screens, users sometimes unleash negativity without considering its real-world implications. As noted by Gonzalez, 16% of high school students reported experiencing cyberbullying—an alarming statistic highlighting the pervasive nature of online harassment. Unlike in-person confrontations, these digital altercations often lack resolution, leaving victims grappling with diminished self-confidence and feelings of worthlessness (Gonzalez).

Then there's the concept of echo chambers, where one's social media feeds become a loop of similar thoughts and opinions. By surrounding ourselves with like-minded individuals, we unintentionally limit our exposure to diverse perspectives—a practice known to promote groupthink. This phenomenon stifles individual thinking and innovation, leading us to conform rather than challenge prevailing beliefs.

But fear not! Not everything about social media is doom and gloom. Processing interactions positively begins with building supportive communities that appreciate authenticity over curated perfection. Behind every image is an untold story of bloopers and struggles. Sharing candid moments fosters genuine connections free from the facade of perfectionism.

It's essential to prioritize mental health amidst this digital chaos. Taking back your power involves setting boundaries on screen time and curating content that uplifts rather than compares. Engage in offline activities that nourish the soul—read a book, go for a walk, or breathe. Embrace the joy of being present without constantly seeking validation from a virtual crowd.

An effective strategy to manage the influence of external opinions is practicing gratitude. Start by acknowledging aspects of your life or yourself that bring happiness. Gratitude shifts focus from what others think to appreciate what genuinely counts. When bombarded with criticism or negative feedback, use it as an opportunity for growth. Instead of internalizing harsh words, assess their validity and decide if any constructive insights exist before discarding the rest.

The earlier mentioned guideline-based strategy highlights the importance of reinforcing positive affirmations when navigating social media. Remind yourself that numbers don't define worth; kindness does. Surround yourself with those who celebrate your achievements, regardless of size, and encourage open dialogues about insecurities.

Cultivating resilience against online influences requires conscious effort. It's crucial to remember that everyone presents edited versions of themselves on social media—yes, even the influencers with seemingly perfect lives. We reclaim control over our narratives by focusing less on how many people approve of us online and more on nurturing genuine relationships.

Strategies For Authentic Living Online

Picture this: You're scrolling through your social media feed, where everyone appears to be living their best lives. Perfect vacations, impeccable outfits, flawless skin—it's the norm. But here's a little secret that few people openly discuss: it's mostly smoke and mirrors. Recognizing the gap between our real lives and those postcard-perfect portrayals online can liberate us from the pressure of striving for unattainable perfection.

In our quest to present our ideal selves, we often forget that what we see on social media isn't always the truth. While these platforms offer windows into others' lives, they also function as highly edited highlight reels. A snapshot of a friend's vacation or a celebrity's polished appearance can often lead us to compare ourselves unfavorably. "Why don't I look like that?" or "Why aren't my experiences as exciting?" are questions many of us ask without realizing the role editing plays in crafting these images. It's a bit like comparing an unedited behind-the-scenes clip to the final movie cut—it's just not the same reality.

Understanding what is genuine versus altered online can guide us toward embracing self-acceptance. Remember the last time you snapped that 'perfect' selfie? Admit it, there were probably twenty other shots that didn't cut. Filters and editing tools allow us to alter reality, presenting a more idealized version to the world. It might feel good temporarily, but maintaining this illusion is exhausting over time. Instead, allowing ourselves to embrace our authentic selves—even the unfiltered parts—promotes self-acceptance. When we stop seeking external validation and start appreciating who we are, our flaws and all, our focus shifts from competing with others to building confidence within ourselves.

Consider the journey of distinguishing inspiration from envy when consuming online content. Inspiration is like a gentle nudge, motivating us to improve or try something new. Envy, on the other hand, can trap us in a cycle of comparison and dissatisfaction. The trick is interpreting what we see if someone's achievements inspire you to pursue your goals, extraordinary! But if it makes you feel less than, it might be time to reassess your relationship with social media. Ask yourself, "Am I motivated by admiration, or am I letting jealousy cloud my view?" Cultivating a mindset focused on growth over competition can transform how we engage with digital content.

Celebrating the unedited self is a powerful tool for building confidence and promoting authenticity. It sounds simple, but showing up as your true self, both online and offline, can feel daunting in a world keen on polish and perfection. Imagine posting a picture without a filter or sharing a story without embellishment; it takes courage. Yet, this openness invites others to connect with who you are, creating spaces for genuine interactions. It's akin to meeting a friend who's always candid and sincere—their authenticity draws you in because there's no façade, just the comfort of knowing they are real.

Creating such spaces leads to a ripple effect, encouraging others to follow suit. When one starts celebrating their raw, unedited moments, it inspires others to do the same. Recently, actress Pamela Anderson decided to expose herself to the media without makeup for this exact reason. Social media transforms from a platform dominated by unrealistic standards to one that fosters human connection, empathy, and empowerment. This shift builds individual confidence and challenges societal norms, pushing forward a narrative where being true to oneself is celebrated and respected.

So, how can we practice authenticity in a world teeming with filters and edits? Here are a few guidelines to help you get started:

1. Pause Before Posting: Take a moment to consider why you're sharing something. Is it to impress others or because it genuinely brings you joy?

2. Curate Wisely: Follow accounts that uplift and inspire rather than trigger insecurities. Your feed should reflect your interests and values.

3. Engage Honestly: Be sincere when interacting online. Commenting positively and constructively encourages others to do the same.

4. Set Boundaries: If you feel overwhelmed, limit your exposure to social media. Taking breaks can recharge your mental well-being.

5. Reflect On Gratitude: Focus on what you appreciate about your life outside the digital realm to ground yourself in reality.

Final Thoughts

Alright, let's wrap this up with a chuckle or two. Imagine you're on social media, scrolling through a parade of impeccable lives, maybe feeling like you're the only one whose morning coffee spills more than it pours elegantly into the cup. Yet, as we've explored, those filtered images are just digital magic tricks—like trying to convince yourself that kale chips taste better than potato chips (they don't, but hey, we try). Social media tends to show us sliced moments of perfection but don't let them pixel-paint your self-worth. Behind every glamorous influencer and flawless selfie lies a pile of outtakes and failed attempts that could fill entire blooper reels. When you peel back the layers of Photoshop and filters, remember: everyone else is just as human as you, complete with bad hair days and awkward dance moves.

Before we hit "log off" on this chapter, think about this: authenticity might seem like a daring challenge amidst all the sequined snapshots online, but it's worthwhile. Imagine stepping onto the social stage without the masks, sharing those honest, bedhead-included snippets of life. Celebrate the beauty in being authentic because that's where genuine connections bloom. When we laugh at our silly mishaps, post something a little raw, or dare to be ourselves sans filter, we invite others to do the same. So, embrace your life's wonky, imperfect, and occasionally chaotic bits. Remember, it's okay if not everything looks like it belongs on the cover of Vogue; sometimes, the funniest stories come from when things went hilariously awry. In this world of perceived perfection, let authenticity be your compass—because, trust me, the real you is pretty awesome without a filter.

CHAPTER 9

SETTING PERSONAL BOUNDARIES

Setting personal boundaries is like fitting yourself into a suit—it's tailored, comfortable, and essential to safeguarding your well-being. Instead of fabric, these suits are made from invisible threads that help weave your mental peace and self-love into every interaction you have. Establishing boundaries isn't about building walls; it's like crafting a flexible picket fence that breathes with the breeze of life's fickle nature. Whether you're dodging your friend's "moving" party or managing work expectations, setting boundaries is crucial for maintaining peace in the chaotic world we call life. Think of it as your personalized life GPS, keeping you on the right track while ensuring you don't stumble off a cliff when Google Maps decides to nap.

In this chapter, you'll embark on a witty adventure exploring those borderlines between being a people-pleaser extraordinaire and a Zen master with impeccable energy reserves. You'll start by identifying your boundary alarms—those subtle hints your body sends when someone asks too much. By learning to detect these signals, you prevent stress and resentment from having a field day at your expense. Then, gear up for some relationship auditing, where you pull out your trusty metaphorical magnifying glass to see which social interactions drain you faster than your phone's battery during a Netflix binge. We'll also spot sneaky emotional triggers that send you spiraling, equipping you to dodge stress landmines like a pro. Reflective moments await as we rewind the tape on past experiences, drawing lessons without self-chiding and upgrading our internal settings to better align with current needs. This chapter guides you to embracing your rightful space, equipped with humor, self-awareness, and boundaries sharp enough to slice through societal pressures. So grab a comfy seat and a curious mind—we're about to redefine living at peace with yourself and others.

Identifying Personal Limits

Recognizing that uneasy feeling in the pit of your stomach is often your internal boundary alarm sounding off. You've felt it before, right? Someone's asking too much of you, or maybe you've stayed out longer than planned. That discomfort? It's like your body waving a little red flag, saying, "Hey, something's not quite right here!" Paying attention to this sensation can be a vital first step toward recognizing where your limits lie. When we ignore these signals, they become louder and more insistent, eventually morphing into stress or resentment. So, give that discomfort a voice—it's telling you exactly where your boundaries might need some reinforcement.

Next up on our boundary expedition is a bit of relationship auditing. Picture yourself equipped with a trusty energy meter, assessing who might be depleting your power reserves. Friends, neighbors, that overly chatty barista—who leaves you feeling lighter, and who feels like an unplanned trip to the dentist? We've all been there, exchanging polite nods while secretly plotting escape routes from energy vampires. The trick is figuring out which relationships leave you supercharged and which could use a sturdy fence. Knowing where your energy drains occur helps pinpoint precisely where those boundaries should pop up—like assembling your protective force field.

While we're in detective mode, why stop at relationships? Let's talk triggers. No, not the ones on water guns—the emotional kind! Specific situations or behaviors can send us spiraling into irritation or anxiety faster than you can say "stress ball." Identifying these sneaky triggers empowers you to anticipate potential stressors with the precision of a psychic superhero. Knowing what sets you off is critical to setting preemptive boundaries, whether it's the sound of your mother-in-law's ringtone or the mere thought of attending another team-building retreat. By identifying these culprits, you'll navigate life's stress minefield more gracefully without spontaneous combustion.

Now, let's rewind the tape and reflect on past experiences. Have you ever had a moment where you thought, "Wow, I wish I'd spoken up back then"? Replaying these scenes isn't about self-chiding but mining moments for wisdom. These past scenarios—where boundaries were as absent as my motivation for morning jogs—can offer remarkable insights into your current needs. Did that overcommitment lead to burnout? Maybe that time you agreed to dog-sit resulted in unforeseen chaos. Understanding these episodes encourages boundary tuning, ensuring you're better prepared for similar situations in the future.

So, let's grab a cup of feel-good beverage and consider why reflecting on these experiences matters. It ensures your boundaries aren't just ancient relics but adaptable guidelines that evolve as you do. It's like upgrading your phone's operating system, but it's only more relaxed because you're troubleshooting life itself. Acknowledging where you faltered, you fine-tune your internal compass, gaining better clarity on what makes you tick. This ongoing learning process from your history enhances self-awareness and boosts your mental resilience in facing future challenges.

Communicating Assertively

When it comes to setting personal boundaries, clarity is critical. It's like assembling a barbeque without the instructions—things can get confusing quickly. One effective way to express your boundaries is using 'I' statements. Picture this: instead of blaming someone and saying, "You never listen to me," try framing it as "I feel unheard when I don't get a response." This approach shifts the focus from blame to how you feel, which is healthier and less likely to put the other person on defense. Besides, who wants to deal with defensive posturing? We're here for constructive conversation, not a jousting match!

Another trick up your sleeve should be directness. Imagine you're a GPS guiding someone; vague directions won't help them reach their destination. Similarly, being unclear about what you're comfortable with is a recipe for misunderstandings. Being direct means expressing precisely what you mean, so there's no room for misinterpretation. Say just that if you need peace after 9 PM! Don't allude to it in mysterious smoke signals.

Now, let's talk timing. Recognizing the right moment to discuss boundaries can make or break a conversation. You wouldn't want to start this discussion during a heated argument or when the other person is visibly stressed unless you fancy turning it into a WWE smackdown. Instead, aim for a calm setting when both parties are relaxed. Think of it as choosing the perfect moment to plant a seed— it's more likely to grow if the conditions are just right.

Of course, none of this will work out well if we aren't listening actively. Active listening is like giving the other person an all-access VIP pass to a concert where they're the main act, complete with empathy and attention. By truly listening, you value their perspective, which encourages mutual respect. However, this doesn't mean agreeing with everything they say; it's more about understanding their viewpoint. This simple act can work wonders for reinforcing your boundaries while acknowledging theirs.

And let's not forget the secret sauce to these conversations: humor. Lightening the mood doesn't mean belittling the seriousness of the topic but rather making it more digestible. Just remember, there's no harm in sprinkling a little wit here and there as you navigate these discussions. For instance, when explaining why you can't house a friend's pet llama for the weekend, humor can help disarm any potential tension.

Something else worth noting is confidence. Building self-confidence is like assembling a sturdy fort around your boundaries. The higher your self-esteem, the easier it becomes to convey your limits. Like a motivational cheese grater, self-help books, affirmations, and surrounding yourself with positive influences can aid in maintaining consistency with your boundaries. Let's face it: nobody wants their boundary fortress to crumble at the slightest gust of wind.

For those feeling unsure, baby steps are just fine—start small! Practice setting boundaries in situations that involve low risks. You could establish a boundary with a barista who consistently gets your coffee order wrong. Consequential? Perhaps not. But every little victory prepares you for more significant challenges, like addressing workplace dynamics without fear of becoming the office villain. And hey, once you've gained some mileage, seeking the guidance of a coach or therapist specializing in communication might also unlock new levels of confidence.

Consistency pairs right alongside practice—think iced tea and sunny afternoons. Consistently enforcing boundaries helps solidify them over time. A word of caution, though: hold others accountable just as you expect them to respect yours. It's about practicing what we preach. But don't fret, even if enforcing boundaries feels awkward initially; with time, this newfound strength can become second nature, almost like riding a bicycle without training wheels.

Ultimately, knowing how to express your boundaries fosters healthy relationships wherein respect reigns supreme, like an unspoken agreement between superheroes and villains to clash only in spectacular settings. Amidst all this, remember these talks are a two-way street—you can't steer the conversation by controlling both lanes. Find balance through assertiveness and empathy because nothing strengthens bonds better than genuine understanding and shared respect.

Saying No With Confidence

In today's bustling world, the simple yet profound act of saying "no" often takes a backseat. Getting swept up in the endless tide of commitments and requests is easy, leaving little room for personal space and mental peace. However, embracing the power of "no" is not just about turning down an invitation or declining to take on additional responsibilities; it's about reclaiming your energy, safeguarding your time, and fortifying your commitment to self-care.

Imagine your time and energy as a limited resource. Each time you say "yes" when you mean "no," you're chipping away at that reserve. By embracing the power of "no," you protect these vital resources, allowing yourself to focus on what truly matters: your well-being. Self-care isn't a luxury; it's a necessity, and saying "no" is one of its most essential practices. Whether skipping a social event that's more obligation than joy or setting boundaries at work to maintain a healthy work-life balance, each "no" is a step towards prioritizing yourself.

Of course, the art of refusal isn't merely about saying the word itself. It's also about how you say it. Practicing assertive refusal means arming yourself with the tools to reject requests politely yet firmly. Many people dread the thought of disappointing others and, therefore, shy away from refusal, fearing confrontation or negative repercussions. But here's a secret: mastering the skill of assertive communication can alleviate that anxiety.

Instead of flat-out "no," try expressions that convey your decision with kindness. For instance, "I appreciate the offer, but I must prioritize my current obligations." Such expressions help maintain relationships while respecting your boundaries. The truth is most people admire honesty and clarity over half-hearted commitments. When you communicate your limits openly, it often leads to stronger connections built on mutual respect.

One intriguing aspect of setting boundaries is the emotional baggage that sometimes accompanies the ride—guilt and fear. Fear of letting others down or being perceived as selfish can be overwhelming. But recognizing these emotions for what they are is the first step toward diminishing their hold over your decisions. It's perfectly normal to feel guilt when asserting your boundaries. Remembering yourself that these feelings don't dictate your actions is crucial. Whenever you acknowledge guilt or fear without caving into it, you reduce its influence over your life.

Picture this: you've said "no" to an extra project at work because you knew it would stretch you too thin. Initially, guilt may whisper doubts in your ear. But as you enjoy a peaceful evening with loved ones instead, the benefits of your choice become clear. Celebrating such decisions doesn't just reinforce the value of maintaining personal boundaries—it bolsters confidence and self-respect. Each successful assertion of your limits is a testament to your growth and boosts your self-esteem.

Setting and maintaining boundaries is akin to planting seeds of empowerment. As you nurture these seeds through consistent practice, you'll notice a transformation in how you perceive yourself and interact with the world. Celebrating those moments when you've upheld your boundaries—even if only to yourself—turns them into personal development milestones.

Consider how much lighter life feels when you're not burdened by commitments that don't align with your values or needs. There's a certain freedom in trusting yourself to make choices that support your well-being rather than adhere to societal expectations. Each "no" becomes a protective barrier and an affirmation of self-worth. You're telling the world and yourself, "I am worthy of time and peace."

Embracing the power of saying "no" requires a shift in perspective. It's about valuing oneself enough to recognize that your needs deserve attention just as much as those of others. This mindset fosters a healthier relationship with yourself, paving the way for more balanced interactions with those around you.

It's worth noting that fostering this habit won't come overnight, and that's perfectly okay. Change takes time, practice, and compassion toward yourself. There will be moments of doubt or missteps, but each attempt equips you with valuable insights for future encounters.

Imagine living where you feel empowered to decline opportunities that don't serve your goals or passions, where guilt holds no sway over your decisions. By embracing the power of "no, " you're heading in that direction. With each decision, you're crafting a narrative where your voice is respected, your boundaries acknowledged, and your peace preserved.

Reflecting On Boundaries

Setting personal boundaries is like being an artist in the world of self-care. You have a brush, and the canvas is your life. But here's the kicker: it's a constantly evolving masterpiece, not just a once-and-done job. Recognizing that our needs and circumstances are continually changing and regularly reflecting on our boundaries can help us adapt as we grow. This is essential for ongoing personal growth and well-being. You wouldn't wear your winter coat in the summer. Just as we adjust our wardrobes with the seasons, we must routinely check if our lines in the sand need shifting.

Reflecting involves more than just pondering about your past weekend over coffee; it's about asking yourself the tough questions. How did those boundaries serve you when things got challenging? Were they too rigid or perhaps too lax? Think about a time when you felt overwhelmed—possibly your boss thought "urgent" was synonymous with "immediate response," leaving your phone buzzing at all hours. That's a clue that maybe your work-life boundary could use some reinforcement.

Interestingly, feedback from others also plays a crucial role in evaluating our boundaries. Imagine this: Susan at work says she appreciates how you always carve out time for team members without getting frazzled. That's a hint you're doing something right! Constructive feedback can offer fresh perspectives and insights into whether our current boundaries serve us well or require adjustments. It's like getting a sneak peek into how others perceive your boundaries—a way to gauge if they're visible and respected.

Boundaries keep chaos at bay and significantly impact our mental peace. Consider them the Zen Garden of your mind. When maintained, they help you nurture a calm mental state, aiding continual self-improvement. If setting a boundary means saying no to attending yet another committee meeting that eats into your family dinner time, it's a step towards protecting your peace. Understanding this effect encourages us to prioritize boundaries as integral elements of personal development, enhancing our ability to face daily stresses with resilience.

Now, let's talk about the magic of sharing reflections with trusted folks. You've drawn up your boundaries, and now comes the part where you might buzz with nervousness at the thought of voicing them. Yet, communicating these boundaries to friends or loved ones can be a game-changer. It's like having a trusty GPS when wandering through foreign cities. Sharing your experiences and relaying how certain boundaries keep you grounded fortifies personal growth and builds more robust relational support networks. Your best friend may remind you later, "Hey, didn't you say Sundays are your 'me' days?"

When someone truly understands your boundaries, they become allies in maintaining them. Verbalizing the boundaries and rationale behind them confidently reinforces the mindset that prioritizing your needs is not only okay but necessary. This transparency fosters a mutual respect and understanding culture where everyone feels heard and valued.

As life's demands shift, so must our boundaries. Regular reflection ensures we're not stuck using outdated guideposts. Analyzing feedback helps refine those boundaries, turning the noise around us into actionable wisdom. Moreover, realizing the profound connection between established boundaries and inner tranquility nudges us toward consistent self-betterment. The bonus here? Sharing these insights isn't just beneficial; it's essential. Engaging with our trusted circles enriches personal growth journeys and strengthens the support each person offers in their relationships.

Final Insights

Navigating the world of personal boundaries is like mastering an art form—an art filled with hilarious missteps and invaluable lessons. We've wandered through the amusing yet enlightening landscape of identifying limits, energy-vampire relationships, and emotional landmines, discovering that our internal boundary alarms are as accurate as those pesky indigestion pangs after a midnight snack. Establishing these boundaries is crucial, acting like a protective force around your mental peace and self-love. Think of them as the invisible buffer at a concert that saves you from an elbow to the face in a mosh pit. By acknowledging what's draining—or charging—our energy reserves, we can better direct our GPS to navigate life's unpredictable streets without rerouting every five minutes.

As we've ventured through the quirky realities of assertive communication and the art of confidently saying "no," it's clear that setting boundaries isn't about building impossible fortresses but crafting a tailored safety net for your sanity. Sure, it might require awkward conversations and a sprinkle of humor to sweeten the deal, like telling your friend, "The only llama I'm responsible for this weekend is a Dalai Lama podcast." But each "no" is a step closer to embracing self-worth, where guilt and fear are powerless over your decisions. Remember, sharing these aha moments with those we trust transforms potential pitfalls into a footbridge, fostering more meaningful connections. So, here's to drawing lines in the sand that ebb and flow with life's tides, ensuring you ride the waves with less stress and more laughter along the way.

CHAPTER 10

MINDFULNESS IN SELF-LOVE

Mindfulness in self-love is like having your cake and eating it, too—only this time, the cake is a multi-layered masterpiece of awareness and acceptance. Picture yourself in a chaotic day where deadlines loom, and the coffee machine conspires against you. But instead of spiraling into stress mode, you've got this secret weapon tucked away: a mindfulness practice that hits pause on the madness just long enough to breathe. Mindfulness isn't about zoning out or transcending into a Zen state at a meditation retreat. It's as simple as acknowledging and treating your thoughts like clouds floating past a bright blue sky. It's about being fully present and checking in with your inner monologue as if it's your favorite podcast (because sometimes, your brain does have the best stories).

In this chapter, we'll delve into mindfulness as a tool for self-love, minus the fluff and fanfare. We'll uncover how being present can help you dodge those pesky societal judgments like dodging a flying frisbee at the park. You'll explore various tried-and-tested mindfulness techniques—from breathwork to body scan meditations—that help tune out the world's noise, even for a moment. Imagine learning to savor a bite of chocolate as if it's the only thing keeping you tethered to reality; that's the magic we'll dive into. We'll shatter myths circling mindfulness like mosquitoes around a summer barbecue and empower you with practices that fit seamlessly into the hustle and bustle of modern life. By the end, you'll be equipped to face external expectations with newfound resilience and sprinkle self-love into every nook and cranny of your daily routine.

Understanding Mindfulness

Picture this: you're lounging on a lazy Sunday afternoon with no plans and nowhere to be, simply present, savoring the moment. No judgments of what you should or shouldn't be doing, just enjoying your delightful company. That's mindfulness—a superpower we've often forgotten to unleash. Imagine learning to extend this vibe to every day, bringing a gentle awareness to our thoughts and emotions, minus the harsh self-critique. Sounds dreamy for boosting self-love, right? So, let's dive in!

Mindfulness is like that old friend who always lets you vent without judgment, constantly reminding you that you're enough just as you are. It's about being engrossed in the here and now, acknowledging your inner monologue without letting it spiral into a full-blown drama scene. According to (Mindful Staff, 2020), we all possess mindfulness—it's innate and accessible anytime once we unlock it.

Though mindfulness might seem like a buzzword parading around in linen pants, its roots run deep through the annals of history. Historically, mindfulness has centered around self-acceptance, which makes perfect sense. How can you truly love yourself if you're unaware of who you are or continually critique yourself with reckless abandon?

Through the ages, people have used mindfulness to foster acceptance of themselves—flaws, quirks, and all. This practice of gently observing one's internal landscape has stood the test of time precisely because it's relevant today, especially with societal pressures trying to mold us into imperfect beings. When you nurture self-acceptance, you build a foundation of self-love so solid that even the judgments of others can't shake it.

Then there's the little-known perk of emotional regulation—mindfulness is like a trusty sidekick in managing reactions to external chaos. Life throws curveballs, like your boss's unexpected critique or an accidental double-tap on your ex's Instagram vacation photo. You build a buffer against these disruptions by engaging in regular mindfulness activities, thanks to enhanced emotional control. You learn to respond rather than react, savoring that sweet pause where choice lives.

This isn't some pop psychology mumbo-jumbo; it's grounded in science. Mindfulness helps steer your emotional ship through turbulent waters by promoting balance and resilience. Knowing they don't define you, you become more adept at handling external judgments gracefully—and maybe even a smirk.

Now, about those myths swirling around like rogue tumbleweeds. Some folks believe that effective mindfulness demands hours-long meditation marathons, during which you must clear your mind of all thoughts. Cue eye rolls! This myth needs busting pronto. Mindfulness can begin with something as simple as a few conscious breaths while waiting for your coffee to brew. Talk about efficiency!

Short practices fit seamlessly into busy lives, offering profound benefits without needing a Himalayan retreat. Remember, the quality of the awareness, not the duration of the training, counts. Anyone—even those stuck in traffic or washing dishes—can embrace brief mindful moments throughout their day. Mine comes when I'm taking my morning beach run. I never tire of the sound and power of the ever-changing surf.

While some think mindfulness requires complex rituals, its simplicity is its power. There's no need to morph into a Zen master overnight. Mindfulness is about participation, not perfection, allowing each small step to contribute to nurturing self-love.

Mindful Meditation Techniques

Breath awareness meditation is like giving your mind a cozy blanket and a cup of cocoa—it's calming, comforting, and makes you feel grounded. Picture yourself in the middle of a bustling city, honking cars and people rushing by, but there you are, wrapped in tranquility. This practice involves focusing on your breathing, noticing each inhale and exhale without trying to control it. As simple as it sounds, this technique can work wonders in reducing anxiety and self-doubt. It's like having a secret weapon against the chaos around you. Paying attention to your breath anchors yourself in the present moment, pulling away from nagging thoughts about the past or what-ifs about the future. Imagine telling that internal critic to hike for a few minutes while you enjoy peace.

Now, let's talk about body scan meditation—a real treat for those who've ever felt like a zombie moonwalking through life. This technique encourages you to mentally scan your body from head to toe, tuning into sensations and feelings. Think of it as a mini-vacation where you reconnect with every part of yourself, even that weird twinge in your left shoulder you've ignored. The best part? You don't have to fix anything. This isn't a DIY project—observe and appreciate. During the process, you might become aware of tension you didn't even realize you were carrying, like that backpack full of bricks called stress. But here's the kicker: recognizing these sensations cultivates acceptance and appreciation for your body. Like a beloved old sweater, you're acknowledging its flaws.

If body scanning feels too much like a medical procedure, how about indulging in some daydreaming with visualization meditation? This one lets you be a director of your mental movie. Visualization involves creating positive images in your mind, reinforcing how fabulous you are—or could be if you weren't still wearing pajamas at 3 PM. Create scenes where you're thriving, feeling confident, happy, and loved. Guided imagery helps reshape those pesky negative self-perceptions into something like, "Darn right, I'm awesome!" Picture yourself achieving goals, standing tall, meeting challenges gracefully—and looking fabulous. Visualization is not just about escaping reality; it's about planting seeds of positivity that slowly sprout into genuine confidence.

Have you ever tried walking meditation? It's like taking mindfulness for a stroll—literally! This isn't about power-walking or getting your steps in; walking meditation combines movement with mindful attention. It's particularly delightful because it takes a seemingly mundane task and transforms it into an opportunity for self-love. Imagine each step as a gentle pat on your own back, reminding you that you're moving forward physically and metaphorically. You focus on the sensation of your feet meeting the ground, the rhythm of your walk, and the world around you. Walking becomes a dance of awareness, helping you connect with the now while embracing the nurturing act of movement. It's an excellent practice for those who find sitting meditation akin to watching paint dry—this gets you out and about while reaping the benefits of mindfulness.

Incorporating these techniques into your routine doesn't require a transformational overhaul. Think of them as little nuggets of gold scattered throughout your day. Start with a short breath awareness session during your morning coffee break. Take five minutes to do a body scan before bed, letting go of the day's stresses. Infuse your afternoon with visualization, picturing success before tackling tasks. And if you can, swap your next hurried commute for a relaxed, mindful walk. Each practice brings presence, kindness, and love toward yourself, ultimately enriching your self-love journey.

Remember, you're not striving for perfection in this practice—no one expects you to levitate after two breaths. Mindfulness is about gently guiding yourself back to love and compassion whenever you wander off to Critic Land. This playful yet profound approach to meditation allows you to break free from the shackles of societal expectations, embracing a whimsical yet heartfelt path to self-acceptance.

Society loves to peddle its ideals, leaving many of us feeling like we're constantly auditioning for a role we'll never quite fit. But guess what? You're already cast in the leading role of your life. These mindfulness meditation techniques help flip the narrative, turning your inner dialogue from "not enough" to "more than enough." You're not just surviving; you're thriving in your unique, imperfect way.

Integrating Mindfulness Daily

Starting your day with a splash of mindfulness is like planting a tiny seed of self-love that flowers throughout the day. Imagine waking up to the chaotic beeping of your alarm and resisting the urge to dive straight into the social media abyss on your phone. Instead, you take a deep breath and focus your attention on the warmth of the sheets, the soft light seeping through the curtains, and perhaps even the comforting aroma of coffee brewing in another room. This pause, this moment of awareness, sets a tone of positivity and intention for your day. It's like putting on a pair of mental glasses that let you see the world through a lens of calm and clarity.

Staying mindful during the hustle and bustle of the day can feel like trying to hold onto a soap bubble. One minute, you're zen-like and composed; the next, you're stressing about an email marked "urgent." To keep your mindfulness game strong, think of small reminders or cues to help steer your mind back to the present. Sticky notes on your desk with little affirmations can be like mini pep talks from past you to Future, encouraging a moment of stillness amid chaos. Or consider setting hourly reminders on your phone, not to check tasks off your list, but to breathe deeply and refocus your energy. It's like turning a distraction into a divine reminder of what's essential—your peace of mind.

Then there's the delicious practice of mindful eating—a delightful way to show love to yourself and those taste buds! Usually, meals become pit stops between tasks, mindlessly gobbled before the next scheduled item. But what if we took a different approach? When you sit down to eat, first notice the vibrant colors and aromas dancing off your plate. Please take a moment to express gratitude for the nourishment before you, whether it's a humble sandwich or an elaborate dish you whipped up. Then, as you chew, savor each bite slowly, letting your senses travel through textures and flavors. This isn't merely a gastronomic pleasure; it's a celebration of nourishing yourself physically and emotionally, honoring your health priorities without yielding to external pressures about diet or body image.

As the sun sets, it's time to unwind and reflect on your day. Evening reflections act similarly to bookends for your daily journey of self-awareness. Amidst Netflix binging or scrolling through memes, take a moment to acknowledge all you've accomplished today. Even if the victory is as tiny as finally sorting out the junk drawer or remembering to water the plant waving at you for months, give yourself a pat on the back. Reflecting isn't about critiquing what you didn't achieve; it's about recognizing your efforts and progress, however incremental they might be. In doing so, you're telling yourself, "Hey, I see you. You're awesome." It turns sleep into a well-deserved reward instead of an exhausted collapse.

Dispelling Myths Around Mindfulness

In the colorful world of self-love, mindfulness often takes center stage, but there are quite a few myths floating around that can deter people from fully embracing this powerful practice. Discover these common misconceptions and clear the path toward healthier understanding and practice.

First, there's a myth that mindfulness is about emptying your mind — imagine sitting cross-legged with a serene smile, achieving nothingness. Sounds exhausting. Well, here's the reality check: mindfulness is not about shoving away every thought you have. It's about engaging with them in a conscious, non-judgmental way. Think of it as inviting your thoughts over for tea rather than locking them out of the house. By paying attention to your thoughts, you're promoting more apparent self-awareness. This presence helps you understand yourself better and make peace with those quirky inner dialogues rather than running from them.

Then there's the belief that effective mindfulness practice resembles advanced origami — complex and intricate. But fear not, because mindfulness isn't about mastering brain-bending techniques; it's as simple as focusing on your breath or observing the sensations in your body. You don't need to chant mantras while balancing on one leg atop a mountain. Even amid life's chaos, you can sprinkle mindfulness into everyday activities like brushing your teeth or sipping your morning coffee by simply being present in the moment. It's about starting small and making it manageable, not another item on a never-ending to-do list.

Another misconception is that mindfulness is exclusively reserved for spiritually enlightened yogis. The truth is that mindfulness opens its doors wide to everyone, regardless of whether you can touch your toes or recite sutras. You don't have to be a Zen master to benefit from mindfulness. It's an equal-opportunity practice that welcomes anyone willing to try it. Whether you're a busy parent juggling school lunches or a techie working through code, mindfulness can fit snugly into whoever you are and whatever you do.

Myth number four on our hit list is that it takes ages to see any benefits from mindfulness. Picture yourself grinding away at mindfulness exercises for decades like a monk in a Hollywood movie, waiting for enlightenment to finally knock. The reality? Positive effects can reveal themselves surprisingly quickly. Some studies have shown improvements in well-being and focus after a single session. So, grab a chair (or not), get comfy, and know you're already on the right path, even if you're only five minutes into your first practice.

Finally, let's bust the myth that mindfulness leaves you blissed 24/7. As delightful as constant euphoria sounds, it's not the point. Mindfulness teaches you to roll with whatever feelings show up. There will be days when meditation feels as relaxing as a warm bath and others where it's like untangling Christmas lights. Both are perfectly normal experiences. The trick is to accept whatever happens without judgment and return your attention to the present moment. Over time, this skill brings more significant presence and peace into your life as muscle strengthens with repetition.

Addressing these myths isn't just about clearing misconceptions; it's about encouraging more people to integrate mindfulness into their lives. When mindfulness is demystified and seen for what it truly is—an accessible, practical tool for everyone— it becomes a powerful ally in nurturing self-love and resilience. More folks might think, "Hey, I can do this," and go on to transform their relationships with themselves.

Final Thoughts

As we wrap up this mindful adventure, let's take a step back (mindfully) and reflect on what we've unraveled about nurturing self-love. We delved into how mindfulness is your ever-present cheerleader, one that doesn't just wave pom-poms but helps you silence that pesky inner critic by living in the moment. No more letting societal pressures mold us into airbrushed versions of ourselves! With ancient roots and modern flair, practicing mindfulness enables you to be unapologetically you, shaking off external judgments like water off a duck's back while building a fortress of self-acceptance.

So, here's the takeaway: mindfulness doesn't require a Himalayan retreat or hours of meditation to boost your self-worth—it's all about those precious snippets in everyday life. Whether you're anchoring yourself with breath awareness, reveling in a body scan, or visualizing success in your PJs, these presence bits enhance your self-love journey. Even mundane tasks, like walking from your desk to the fridge, can morph into moments of mindful magic. Let's shake off any myths slowing you down because who needs a ticket to Critic Land when you've got a VIP pass to Thrivingville? Now, sprinkle some mindfulness over your days like confetti, and watch that self-love blossom!

CHAPTER 11

FINDING HUMOR IN COMPARISONS

Finding humor in comparisons is like adding color to an otherwise monochrome picture. We all know the scenario: scrolling through social media, surrounded by posts of vacation pics that make the Maldives look pedestrian or fitness updates that might as well come with their trainer tucked inside the comments section. It's easy to find ourselves swept away by self-doubt and envy, but injecting humor can offer a life vest. Picture this: instead of sinking into thoughts like "Why don't I have a six-pack?" you laugh it off, imagining your abs as over-enthused couch potatoes too comfortable to reveal themselves. This comedic twist doesn't just lighten the mood—it shifts perspective, turning the relentless comparison game on its head.

As we navigate the quirky landscape of comparisons, this chapter takes readers on a humorous journey through the unexpected allies of laughter and light-heartedness. The text beckons readers to explore funny anecdotes of extreme comparative follies, where one-upmanship resembles a sitcom more than real life. You'll encounter tales of people turning daily missteps into comic gold, all while discovering how these laughable moments teach us about embracing our unique quirks. From the art of creating a 'Comparison Calendar' to rebranding mishaps as delightful features, the pages unravel strategies for harnessing humor for self-betterment. By diving into playful narratives and whimsical scenarios, you'll find that comparing becomes not a thief of joy but a comical companion on the journey to self-acceptance.

Recognizing Comparison Traps

Social media can often seem like a mirage of perfection in an age dominated by endless scrolling and double taps. Just a few minutes online, you're swimming in images of flawless vacations, inspirational bodies, and gourmet meals plated like art. These snapshots create a comparison trap—sticky snares of unrealistic standards that make us question our lives. Platforms like Instagram have famously been identified as the most harmful to mental health because they foster these false comparisons (Warrender & Milne, 2020). They propagate an illusion where everyone except you appears to be living their best life. It's crucial to remember that what we see on these platforms is an edited highlight reel rather than a reflection of reality. Recognizing this mirage is the first step to minimizing its impact.

One practical guideline for tackling these social media traps is to be mindful of your triggers. Pay attention to which posts or accounts consistently bring you down or ignite that spark of envy. Consider unfollowing those sources to create a healthier online environment. Remembering yourself amid all this digital noise is essential: "Don't compare someone's outside to your inside." The personas on social media are often crafted to attract attention, not to mirror real life. Practicing gratitude is another powerful antidote to these feelings; focus on the good in your life instead of what's missing.

Spotting the instinct to compare involves taking a scuba dive into self-awareness. This impulse doesn't just appear out of nowhere; it's often rooted in our insecurities. Our minds are wired to evaluate ourselves against others, but doing so without mindfulness can lead us down a dark rabbit hole. Anxiety and dissatisfaction bubble up when our internal dialogue goes unchecked. Mindfulness practices, like meditation or journaling, can help manage these emotions by bringing them into plain view. By identifying and acknowledging our inadequacies, we empower ourselves to challenge their validity and lessen their intensity.

A practical guideline here is to cultivate a routine of self-reflection. Regularly setting aside time to explore your thoughts and feelings can reveal underlying insecurities, triggering comparison. For instance, asking yourself why a particular person's success bothers you may uncover personal aspirations or fears. Understanding these reactions allows for more compassionate self-dialogue and reduces the tendency to measure oneself against others.

The instinctual comparison game often leads to cognitive dissonance, where conflicting beliefs cause discomfort. You might believe you're successful in your career until you see a peer's seemingly meteoric rise. Suddenly, your sense of accomplishment feels diminished. This inner conflict breeds turmoil, feeding into the notion that you're somehow lacking. Cognitive dissonance is uncomfortable, but it also presents an opportunity. Acknowledging these feelings can motivate positive change if approached with curiosity rather than judgment. Instead of dwelling on perceived failures, use them as stepping stones to reassess goals and values.

To offset this dissonance, consider flipping the narrative. Instead of fixating on others' achievements, celebrate your milestones, no matter how small. This shifts focus from external validation to internal satisfaction, helping alleviate the tension between reality and fantasy.

Enter the whimsical 'Comparison Calendar.' Imagine jotting down daily wins—from getting through Monday without needing extra coffee to finally nailing that yoga pose without toppling over. By documenting achievements, however mundane, you begin to build a repertoire of personal victories. This playful practice fosters a light-hearted approach to failure as well. Maybe you burnt dinner the night before; it's okay; write it down and laugh at it! Humor softens the edges of disappointment and transforms setbacks into merely funny footnotes in one's journey.

Here are some guidelines for creating your Comparison Calendar. Start by setting realistic expectations and select achievable goals weekly. Each day, record something positive you've accomplished or any 'failure' that taught you a lesson. Allow humor to weave through these entries, reflecting on how trivial many comparisons genuinely are. Over weeks, this calendar becomes a testament to growth, reminding you that life's adventures are about progress, not perfection.

Laughing At The Absurdity

We all know those moments when comparisons seem to take control of our lives, and it's an all-too-familiar scenario. Picture this: a friend gets a promotion, buys a new car, or maybe even posts an envy-inducing vacation picture on social media, and suddenly, you find yourself spiraling into a myriad of self-judging thoughts. It's as if we've entered a bizarre world where everyone competes for the same imaginary prize – a place where humor can play a crucial role in saving our sanity.

To highlight the humorous side of these comparison tendencies, let's dive into some funny stories about extreme comparisons that remind us of their absurdity. Imagine running into someone who has taken inventory of every aspect of their life solely to outdo their neighbor—a dangerous and hilarious competition. You'll hear these people say, "Oh, you climbed Mount Everest? I once climbed the metaphorical mountain of doing my taxes two weeks early." Such tales showcase the lengths people go to win this ultimate game of 'I've-Achieved-More-Than-You,' offering a good chuckle while reminding us that we are not alone in these quirky thought patterns.

Another tool in our comedic arsenal is the meme culture, which perfectly encapsulates how society's comparisons are often hilariously exaggerated. Through absurd and wildly unexpected juxtapositions, memes create shared laughter, highlighting societal standards for the ridiculous constructs they often are. For example, memes showing elaborate skincare routines next to images of raccoons rifling through garbage underscore the amusing reality versus expectation gap many of us feel. They provide a moment of levity, reminding us that we're all just trying to navigate life, sometimes with questionable success.

Taking a step further into the realm of humor, imagine participating in the 'Comparison Olympics,' where competitors vie for gold in such categories as 'Most Unnecessary Gadget Purchased Just Because a Neighbor Had It' or 'Fastest Time Falling Asleep While Stalking Someone's Vacation Photos Online.' Envisioning events like these sheds light on how laughably trivial many of our competitive urges genuinely are. Turning our focus from genuine achievements to these contrived competitions allows us to see how superficialities often dictate our actions. This imaginary event is a humorous guideline, encouraging readers to reflect on real priorities and the oft-overlooked joys outside the comparison-driven hustle.

Laughter, in its essence, can be one of the most unifying emotions. Sharing a chuckle over what might initially seem like a personal setback or difference welcomes others to join in and creates camaraderie. It highlights the commonality of human experience, underlining that missteps and quirks aren't weaknesses—they're collective proof of our humanity. When we laugh about our imperfections, we acknowledge that trying to meet unrealistic standards isn't worth the stress. Instead, we stretch our wingspan beyond the narrow confines of societal expectations, flying toward a horizon rich with authenticity and relatable stories.

Choosing Joy Over Envy

In the vast tapestry of human emotions, envy is a thread that can weave itself all too easily into our daily lives. Yet, with some humor and perspective, we can transform this sometimes-pesky emotion into a source of joy and personal growth. Let's dive into how to turn those moments of green-eyed wonder into opportunities for self-improvement and happiness.

Choosing Joy over Envy: The Gratitude Shift

Gratitude is often touted as one of the most potent antidotes to envy. It's like having your superhero cape—you put it on, and suddenly, everything looks brighter. Focusing on gratitude shifts your perspective from what you lack to what you already have. You start noticing your life's tiny victories and joys, like finding an extra fry at the bottom of your fast-food bag or receiving an unexpected compliment.

To kick-start this gratitude revolution in your life, make it a habit to list three things you're grateful for each day. They don't have to be grand; they must be genuine. Perhaps it's the sound of rain tapping against your window or the feeling of fresh sheets after a long day. By routinely practicing gratitude, you'll discover little room left for envy because you're too busy basking in the glow of your own life's awesomeness. This practice isn't about ignoring other people's successes but appreciating your journey. It's the subtle art of turning "Why not me?" into "Look at what I've got!" (DMS Analytics Consulting, 2024).

Joyful Celebrations

Now, let's talk about the joy of cheering for others. Regularly celebrating the achievements of those around us strengthens bonds and gently nudges comparison out of the spotlight. Consider this:

every time you genuinely celebrate someone else's success, you're chipping away at the barriers envy tries to build between people.

Start small. When a friend gets promoted or hits a personal milestone, celebrate with them. Share their happiness without letting the sneaky comparison demon sabotage the moment. You'll find that this celebration doesn't just bring you closer—it also fills your emotional cup. Over time, these celebrations can create an environment where everyone roots for each other, turning potential competitors into teammates. Pretty soon, you'll find yourself being the biggest cheerleader, pom-poms and all, in a world full of beautiful achievements.

The "Anti-Comparison" Playlist

Ah, music—the universal language of the soul. An 'Anti-Comparison' playlist can be a game-changer in redirecting your thoughts towards positivity. Just as certain tracks can pump you up before a workout, others can soothe your mind and push aside unnecessary comparisons.

Compose a playlist with songs that evoke happiness, motivation, and a sense of chill. Whether it's that catchy pop song, you can't stop humming or an inspiring anthem that makes you want to take on the world, let these tunes work their magic. As you listen, visualize the lyrics wrapping around you like a cozy blanket, guiding your thoughts away from envy and towards a space of joy and self-appreciation. Music can rewire our brains, and an uplifting playlist can be the perfect tool to remind you of your worth.

Visualizing Their Success

Lastly, let's explore the power of visualization—not just for your goals but for how you perceive others' successes. It's easy to fall into a jealousy trap when someone else achieves something you've been striving for. Instead of lamenting their achievements as your own, envision their success and draw inspiration from it. Imagine the steps they took and the effort they invested in, and use them as inspiration for your journey.

This isn't about imitating their path but embracing their success as proof that it's possible. Visualize not with envy but admiration, and let that spark motivate you toward your aspirations. By transforming jealousy into a driving force, you'll begin to see successes—both yours and theirs—as part of a broader narrative of growth and self-love.

Building A Healthier Self-Image Through Humorous Perspectives

Finding humor in comparisons can be a lifeline to a healthier self-image in a world that constantly asks us to measure up. Imagine scrolling through your social media feed and seeing that picture-perfect vacation selfie or an impressive career update from a Facebook friend. It's easy to fall into the trap of comparing your life with theirs, feeling inadequate or left behind. However, humor offers an alternative route—a way to navigate these pressures with grace and self-compassion.

Recognizing when we're slipping into the comparison trap is the first step toward a more compassionate perspective on ourselves. Think about the time your friend posted yet another accomplishment online, and instead of feeling happy for them, you questioned your achievements. Acknowledging this reaction without judgment allows for self-kindness. The next time you catch yourself in such a moment, try framing it with a light-hearted observation about your quirks or misadventures. Humor helps diffuse feelings of inadequacy and opens the door to self-acceptance.

Shared laughter is a powerful tool that fosters camaraderie and diminishes those nagging feelings of being 'less than.' Picture a scenario where you and your friends share stories of past mishaps. When everyone starts laughing at their blunders, it creates an atmosphere of understanding and support. This shared experience connects us, reminding us that we all have shortcomings. Instead of isolating us, laughter brings us together, offering reassurance that nobody's perfect—and that's perfectly okay.

Embracing imperfections with humor enhances self-acceptance and instills pride in our individual stories. Our flaws and foibles are what make us unique. They weave the rich tapestry of personal experiences that shape who we are. By injecting humor into how we view these aspects of ourselves, we shift from hiding imperfections to celebrating them. Next time you try something new and fail spectacularly, consider it another chapter in your ever-growing repertoire of funny anecdotes. Focusing on these light-hearted narratives transforms vulnerabilities into badges of honor, creating a sense of pride in our individuality.

The science supports this approach. Studies indicate that laughter releases hormones like oxytocin (the love hormone), aiding social bonding and trust-building (Lamothe, 2018). Sharing a joke or a funny story about your latest faux pas can bridge gaps and foster connections, making relationships more fulfilling and authentic. When people laugh together, the walls come down. Sharing genuine emotions and thoughts becomes more accessible, leading to deeper, more meaningful interactions (Pike, 2019).

Subtly weaving humor into life's comparisons also helps reframe challenges and ease stress. Consider a workplace mishap: perhaps you tripped while walking into a meeting. Instead of brooding over the embarrassment, a well-timed joke turns it into a memorable, amusing recount rather than a haunting slip-up. Seeing the humor reduces tension and shifts the focus from anxiety to resilience. This reframing emphasizes optimism and adaptability, which are crucial in navigating life's ups and downs.

It's essential to find balance, though, especially when using self-deprecating humor. While poking fun at oneself can defuse awkward situations and enhance emotional well-being, it's vital not to let it become a reflex. If we constantly put ourselves down, it might point to underlying issues that need addressing. Self-deprecation should be used sparingly, ensuring it doesn't chip away at our self-esteem (Pike, 2019).

Developing a healthier self-image by integrating humor into our perceptions allows us to break free from the shackles of constant comparison. Recognizing the humorous side of life's inevitable comparisons and practicing self-compassion unlocks new levels of self-awareness and confidence. We're better equipped to embrace our imperfections and share laughter with others, dissolving barriers and cultivating genuine connections.

The journey to finding humor in comparisons isn't about dismissing ambitions or disregarding growth. Instead, it's about tempering expectations with light-heartedness and viewing challenges as opportunities for joy and community. Doing so enhances our emotional resilience and paves the way for stronger self-acceptance and personal fulfillment.

Final Thoughts

Life can sometimes feel like a giant "Who's better at this?" game fueled by shiny online personas and curated posts. We've gallivanted through tales of comparison traps and the hilarity of keeping up with 'achievements,' all underscored by the whimsical notion that humor is our trusty sidekick. Spotting those moments when we fall into the comparison pit allows us to pause, laugh, and say, "Hey, maybe I'm not perfect, but I've got a funny story or two." Viewing our quirks as quaint little anecdotes instead of flaws, we take a lighter approach to life's little skirmishes against unrealistic measures.

Humor provides a one-size-fits-all life jacket in the wild ocean of social expectations. As we've explored, laughter is the glue that bonds us to others while allowing self-acceptance to blossom amidst the chaos of comparison games. Sharing those imperfect moments with friends doesn't just lessen the sting—it turns them into shared chuckles rather than solitary woes. It's about embracing the absurdity of life's races for imaginary trophies and opting instead to create a community built on shared smiles and mutual understanding. So, here's to laughing off the small stuff, flipping the script on envy, and choosing joy over the relentless pursuit of some elusive perfection.

CHAPTER 12

CRAFTING YOUR NARRATIVE

Crafting your narrative is like being handed a blank canvas and a palette of vibrant colors, with each brushstroke telling a part of your story. It's an opportunity to delve into who you are beyond the limits others may try to impose. Imagine weaving your life into a tapestry that reflects your true self, free from the unyielding expectations that society often casts upon us. This chapter invites you on an adventure of self-discovery, encouraging you to narrate your journey in ways that resonate with your core values, beliefs, and experiences. You'll learn to navigate life's complexities with humor and resilience, turning even the mundane into tales of joy and growth.

In "Crafting Your Narrative," you'll explore techniques to shape your story with creativity and authenticity. The chapter delves into identifying personal themes, those unique threads that run through the fabric of your life, giving it structure and meaning. You'll discover how rewriting past stories can transform embarrassing or awkward moments into powerful scenes of learning and resilience. Creating personal mantras will guide you, lending confidence and clarity as you stroll down your path. Lastly, regular reflection keeps your narrative aligned with your evolving self. With a blend of humor and insightful anecdotes, this chapter empowers you to take charge of your narrative, ensuring it's as colorful and dynamic as you are.

Taking Charge Of Your Narrative

Embarking on the journey of defining and writing your life story can seem as daunting as navigating a labyrinth. Yet, armed with the right tools—such as identifying personal themes, rewriting past stories, creating personal mantras, and engaging in regular reflection—you have all you need to turn this adventure into one filled with humor, resilience, and self-discovery.

The first step is identifying personal themes, which might sound as dry as toast but are, in fact, transformative. Imagine your life as a quilt, each square representing an experience or value that's important to you. These themes are the threadwork holding it together, giving it shape and beauty. Maybe kindness, independence, or innovation are the essential threads of your quilt. Discovering these themes isn't just about listing what you like; it's about discerning which traits resonate so profoundly that they define who you are. A helpful guideline here is to reflect on moments you felt most alive. Were you teaching, exploring, or perhaps nurturing? Jot down these instances; you're one step closer to sewing your unique narrative tapestry.

Once you've pinned down those themes, it's time to rewrite past stories. Let's face it: everyone has a few embarrassing moments they'd rather forget. The trick? Turn them into scenes where you learned something invaluable. Imagine that cringe-worthy job interview where you spilled coffee on yourself as a comedy skit about resilience and handling pressure. Laugh at it, learn from it, and recognize how it molded you into someone who can now ace any challenge without a caffeine mishap. Reframing these experiences transforms them from mere missteps into powerful chapters of growth. Challenge yourself to write down a few of these memories, finding the silver linings and lessons tucked within their folds. My grandmother started down this road and soon had enough chapters to fill a book that she wrote and titled "Many Roads."

Now, let's concoct a Personal Mantra—a tool as ancient as it is effective. A strong mantra acts as your lighthouse during stormy weather. While yoga teachers and meditation gurus talk about deep breathing and "finding your center," you can opt for something more rooted in everyday humor. How about "Stay calm -remember, even the best chefs burn their toast"? Not only does it remind you to stay calm and confident, but it also adds a dash of light-hearted fun. Regularly repeating your mantra helps drown out naysayers and reinforces that you're the captain of this quirky ship called life. (Bay, 2024)

The final ingredient in this storytelling recipe is Engaging in Regular Reflection, a practice that keeps your narrative fresh and true to yourself. Like a backpacker checking their compass, reflecting on your thoughts and actions ensures you're steering toward authenticity. Whether through journaling, doodling, or even voice notes—whatever floats your boat—make it a habit. Set aside a few minutes daily to jot down your thoughts, victories, or even absurd dreams about penguins taking over the world. These reflections provide insight and chart the evolution of your ever-vivid narrative canvas.

Shaping Perceptions Mindfully

Crafting an authentic narrative begins with understanding the delicate balance between your inner self and public persona. This isn't about putting on a mask but ensuring that what you project to the world aligns as closely as possible with your true self while strategically adapting it to various social contexts. Imagine you're starring in your movie; you want the role to be believable but also something you're comfortable portraying. Recognizing the difference between a temporary performance for a specific situation and a permanent alteration of who you are is crucial. Many people fear judgment, often leading them to conform to others' expectations. But knowing when and how to reveal parts of your personality helps preserve your integrity and authenticity.

Social interactions are akin to walking a tightrope—balancing honesty and privacy. You can share your story authentically by setting clear boundaries. Understanding authenticity doesn't mean broadcasting every detail of your life is essential. Instead, it's about being truthful in what you choose to share. For instance, rather than disclosing your personal saga during casual conversations, you might allude to experiences with humor or insight, making sure they relate to the discussion. This sharing not only protects you but makes your exchanges more meaningful.

Humor is a powerful tool in transforming negativity into something positive. It acts as a social lubricant, easing tension and making your story more relatable. Picture yourself stuck in an awkward elevator ride with a stranger—cracking a light-hearted joke about the day's madness can break the ice and create a bond over shared experiences. Humor allows you to frame setbacks as quirky detours, turning potential criticisms into laughable quirks of your unique journey. By embracing wit, you can take charge of how your narrative is perceived, softening any harsh edges life might throw. According to Marwick and Boyd (2011), crafting tweets with personal anecdotes alongside promotional content helps maintain authenticity on platforms like Twitter.

Visual storytelling is another essential component of crafting your narrative. We live in a visually driven world where images speak volumes, often faster than words. Consider using visuals—photos, videos, or even art—to enhance your message. Please consider how Instagram influencers use appealing feeds to convey their stories through aesthetics. They don't just post randomly; each image contributes to an overarching theme of their authentic selves, carefully crafted yet genuine. This doesn't mean creating a façade but selecting visuals that genuinely resonate with you and what you stand for. Storytelling can help you efficiently communicate complex aspects of your identity, leaving a lasting impression.

As we interact with this digital age, presenting ourselves authentically becomes both an art and a science. Social media demands a constant awareness of our audience, creating an ongoing performance. While some view this as daunting, it allows us to consciously reflect on and refine our self-presentation. Just as a sculptor chisels away at a block of marble to reveal a masterpiece, we can also shape our narratives through deliberate presentation choices, using tools available in our modern landscape. Remember, authenticity isn't about laying bare every aspect of yourself; it's about managing perceptions to align with your values while staying grounded in who you are. Santer et al. (2022) emphasize the integration of authenticity and branding to construct a high-quality online persona.

Maintaining authenticity requires embracing a variety of personas suited to different occasions—an approach Generation Z has mastered in their online self-presentation. This flexibility does not equate to being fake; instead, it acknowledges the diversity within us all. Similar to altering your outfit based on event dress codes, adjusting your narrative ensures relevance to the context without compromising your core identity. Selecting which facets to highlight and providing the narrative you tell feels natural to you and your listeners.

Living Authentically

Embracing your true self is like finding that perfectly worn-in pair of jeans—they just fit. At first glance, it may seem easy, but recognizing your authentic voice requires deep introspection. It's about peeling back the layers of external expectations to discover what genuinely resonates with your core beliefs and values

(Butterfly, 2024). Picture yourself standing at a crossroads: one path leading to societal approval, the other to personal fulfillment. Recognizing your authentic voice means choosing the latter, even when the former beckons with glittery promises.

Consider identifying your authentic self, like diving into a pool of cool water on a hot day—refreshing and invigorating. It's not about molding yourself to fit into the swimsuit trends of the season; instead, it's about loving how you swim uniquely. Your authentic voice isn't merely about what you say but how you live, making choices that reflect your true essence. When was the last time you did something solely because it ignited a spark in your soul? That's your authentic voice calling.

As fascinating as authenticity sounds, embracing imperfections adds another hue to your life narrative. Imagine reading a novel where all characters are flawless, and everything unfolds without a hitch—tedious, right? Similarly, our life stories become interesting and relatable through our imperfections. Remember those awkward teenage years or that career mishap that made you feel small? Those moments shape your story's texture. They're not hurdles but stepping stones to life more relatable and genuine (GirlTalkHQ, 2023).

Life's not a glossy magazine cover; it's more like a scrapbook filled with colorful memories, messy glue stains, and crookedly cut photos. Embracing imperfections might mean laughing at your quirks or relishing past mistakes not with regret but with gratitude for the lessons learned. Every flaw tells a tale of resilience, creativity, and growth, adding depth and relatability to your narrative.

Living by your standards requires the courage to turn down a societal script and pick up your pen. Have you ever attended a play and realized you're the lead actor who never got the script? That's life when you follow someone else's narrative. Living by your standards means prioritizing choices that align with personal values rather than chasing societal acceptance (Butterfly, 2024). It's like baking cookies with your recipe rather than following one scribbled by others. Sure, their way might be popular, but the delight of tasting something uniquely yours!

Consider this: while society clamors for conformity, what if you decluttered your space and kept only what truly resonated with you—physically, emotionally, and spiritually? Whether that means pursuing a career less traveled or expressing yourself differently, let your inner compass guide you. After all, when you march to your rhythm, every step becomes a celebration of freedom.

Speaking of celebrations, let's talk about celebrating your journey. Often, we race towards goals, ticking them off like grocery lists, but forget to savor the milestones en route. Celebrating your journey involves acknowledging achievements, no matter how small, and sharing these moments like fireflies illuminating a night. Each milestone inspires community and personal growth (GirlTalkHQ, 2023). What about that moment you felt invincible after achieving a long-held aspiration? Or when a setback became the springboard to discovering a new talent?

Reflect on how far you've come and how each twist and turn contributed to your rich tapestry of experiences. Sometimes, we see ourselves as lone travelers braving unknown paths. Yet, when shared, these experiences can inspire others, nurturing an environment of mutual encouragement. Your life's achievements, both big and small, act as lighthouses for those navigating similar waters.

Enhancing Self-Love Through Narrative

Ever catch yourself starring in life's one-woman (or man) show, where the plot keeps twisting, and you're left wondering who the writer of this crazy script is? Grab your pen because it's time to start crafting your narrative with you as the protagonist. The trick is to shift the lens from societal expectations to cultivating self-love by engaging positively with your personal story. So, let's embark on this journey by recognizing growth, sharing milestones, reinforcing self-esteem, and building a support network.

Let's kick off with a bit of self-reflection. We've all had days when life doesn't seem to cooperate — like getting caught in a rainstorm without an umbrella or tripping before your crush. But here's the plot twist: these challenges are your stepping stones for growth. Think about it. Every cringy presentation and every missed train taught you resilience, didn't they? Recognizing growth means acknowledging that each hurdle has transformed you into a more robust version of yourself. Remember when you were so overwhelmed, and now you laugh at how easy it seems? Yep, that's growth right there, doing its thing, strengthening your narrative without you even knowing.

Now, let's chat about sharing milestones. Imagine your life as a series of social media posts with fewer selfies and more depth. Every achievement, big or small, deserves its moment in the spotlight. Sharing these milestones allows you to celebrate your progress and inspires others. Picture yourself tossing a pebble into a pond; the ripple effect of your achievements can motivate others around you, sparking collective inspiration. A passed exam, a new job, nailing that pasta recipe — each win can inspire someone else to walk a similar path. Plus, let's be honest, who doesn't love a good cheer squad to back them up?

Let's pause here for a moment of real talk about self-esteem. It's often said, "You're your biggest critic," yet we rarely hear, "You're your greatest supporter." It's time to flip that script. Reinforcing self-esteem is all about positive affirmations and self-reflection. Say it with me: "I am awesome." Cheesy? Maybe. Effective? Heck yes! By consistently reciting positive affirmations, you're pumping your self-esteem full of helium — it's bound to lift you higher. Combine this with moments of self-reflection, perhaps during a morning coffee or an evening stroll, and you'll uncover strengths buried beneath those layers of self-doubt. Believe it or not, talking kindly to yourself is serious brain magic.

And speaking of magic, have you ever experienced the wonder of finding your tribe? Building a support network isn't just a buzzword; it's THE word for engaging with people who genuinely appreciate your journey. These folks, whether friends, mentors, or colleagues, become the co-pilots to your aircraft called Life. They're standing by your side, providing a soft landing when you hit turbulence and cheering loudest when you're soaring high. Let's face it: surrounding yourself with like-minded individuals validates your experiences and fuels your pursuit of authenticity. Together, you delight in shared victories and sometimes wallow over shared embarrassments, making life's rollercoaster ride a lot less daunting and more fun.

Before we part ways, remember that weaving humor through this process is pivotal. There is no need to craft a dramatic monologue here; instead, imagine narrating your journey with the same levity and flourish you'd use while recounting an embarrassing slip at the office party. Humor creates room for mistakes, turning them from stumbling blocks into stories you'll giggle at over brunch. It helps to maintain perspective and reminds you that while you may not always control your circumstances, you control how you react to them.

Bringing It All Together

Navigating the highs and lows of life while authoring your own story can feel like starring in a never-ending, offbeat improv show— but you're not just winging it. This chapter has armed you with a toolkit to craft a narrative as unique and vibrant as you are. From pinpointing personal themes that weave through the fabric of your experiences to rewriting those awkward past moments into learning skits, you've got what it takes to make your life's tapestry both colorful and meaningful. Remember, discovering your core themes is like finding those hidden Easter eggs at your grandmother's house—once you see them, everything makes sense, and you can't help but laugh at how they shape each scene. Sprinkle in a personal mantra that keeps you grounded (and maybe a bit cheesy), and you've turned what could be a daunting journey into a delightful masterpiece in progress.

As you continue this adventure, remember that authenticity isn't about broadcasting every plot twist to the world; instead, it's about crafting a storyline that feels genuine to who you are. Whether sharing snippets of your tale with humor or guarding parts that are dearer to you, it's all about striking that balance between openness and privacy. By embracing imperfections and infusing your narrative with wit, you soften life's rough edges, making your journey relatable and entertaining. Visual storytelling adds another layer, allowing you to communicate complex parts of yourself easily. So take a breather, reflect often, and let each step add richness to your ever-evolving story—all while chuckling at the absurdities along the way.

CHAPTER 13

PRACTICING GRATITUDE FOR SELF

Practicing gratitude is like uncovering a hidden superpower, quietly waiting to turbocharge your sense of self and change how you navigate life's inevitable hiccups. Imagine donning a cape of appreciation each morning, making those daily setbacks seem more like gentle nudges than earth-shattering catastrophes. With this newfound perspective, you start seeing yourself as a body moving through chaos and an explorer charting a course through life with laughter and grace. It's about embracing what makes you tick, those quirks and strengths that set you apart from the crowd, and realizing that they are lovable and essential components of who you are. Gratitude invites you on this delightful journey inward, where every reflection in the mirror greets you with a cheerful nod rather than a critical glance.

What awaits in this chapter is a compelling exploration into the art of nurturing gratitude and how it can become the ultimate best friend in bolstering self-compassion. We'll wade through the science of rewiring your brain for positivity with gratitude as your guide, creating a mental landscape that's more roses than thorns. Expect to unearth simple yet powerful practices, like journaling and visualization, that seamlessly weave gratitude into the tapestry of your everyday existence. You'll discover how these practices inoculate you against self-doubt, transforming moments of perceived failure into whimsical stepping stones toward growth. So buckle up because this chapter promises to change how you view gratitude and yourself—through a lens of kindness, humor, and a splash of audacity.

What Gratitude Does For Self-Love

Gratitude is like a pair of magical glasses that lets you see the world—and yourself—in a new light. Imagine waking up each day, slipping on these metaphorical spectacles, and suddenly, all the mediocre things in life become sparkly treasures instead. Before digging for a pair of such glasses, here's a secret: gratitude creates them. It changes how your brain works, building neural pathways that favor positive thinking and shooing away negativity. It's like restructuring your brain to prioritize sunshine and daisies over dark clouds and weeds.

The science behind this transformation starts with our brain's incredible ability to adapt and learn. By consistently practicing gratitude, you're training your brain to focus more on positive aspects than negative ones. This ain't just feel-good fluff; it's grounded in cognitive psychology. For instance, when you're thankful for a friend's kindness or a sunny day, your brain releases dopamine, making you feel good, almost like nature's little happy pill that doesn't require a prescription. Over time, with regular gratitude practice, your brain starts looking for things to appreciate, naturally steering you away from the gloomier side of life.

But the benefits of gratitude don't just stop at mental rewiring. Gratitude also enhances what's known as "cognitive appraisal." Before you roll your eyes and think I'm introducing some posh scientific jargon, let me explain: cognitive appraisal is your brain's knack for evaluating and interpreting situations. When you're grateful, you're better equipped to reflect on experiences without the grating soundtrack of self-doubt and criticism playing in the background. It's like having a calm inner critic who occasionally treats you to a round of applause instead of a heckling session.

Take, for example, a scenario where you've botched a presentation at work. Instead of letting that little voice tell you it was because you're not good enough, gratitude enables you to focus on the effort you poured into preparing. Maybe you'll recognize the skills you've honed through the process, even if the outcome wasn't perfect. This kind of self-reflection fuels personal growth and resilience, turning potential defeats into mere stepping stones. And let's face it, we all need fewer bananas to slip on when life's already tossing coconuts our way.

Beyond changing your perspective and brain chemistry, gratitude acts like a shield—a shiny, emotion-repellent cape against external judgments. In a world where social media can morph into a platform for silently (or not so silently) critiquing everything from your breakfast choice to your political stance, having a buffer helps. You are practicing gratitude, which arms you with emotional resilience. It's like a friendly reminder that your worth doesn't waver based on someone else's opinion shaped by their morning mood or the alignment of the stars.

Imagine gratitude as your cheerleader, following you around, shouting affirmations of greatness every time you trip on self-doubt. Regularly acknowledging what you are grateful for even counteracts the inevitable critiques of others. When you focus on what truly matters—values, friendships, those you love, and more—you create a foundation that's less vulnerable to the slings and arrows of outrageous fortune and those pesky comment threads.

Being aware of your strengths plays a vital role, too. We're often our harshest critics, quick to beat ourselves up for flaws while glossing over accomplishments. Gratitude gently nudges us toward appreciating our strengths. Recognizing what you excel at reduces the tendency to dwell on weaknesses. Think about it: if you were to list three things you admire about yourself each morning, you'd build an impressive stockpile of confidence over time. Self-criticism may still pop by for an occasional visit, but it's less likely to eat you out of the house and at home.

There's something profoundly warming and reassuring about pausing now and then to pat yourself on the back for a job well done or simply for navigating another day. It's like holding a warm cup of cocoa before a cozy fire, savoring the feeling of self-appreciation. Being kind to ourselves in this way nurtures a sense of inner security, allowing us to take risks and embrace opportunities without fear of failure.

Simple Gratitude Exercises

Let's be honest. Gratitude sometimes feels like one of those things people tell us to do but never actually explain how to make it work in the real world. So, let's break it down into bite-sized exercises that fit into our busy lives and help us love ourselves a little more in the process.

First up, we have Daily Gratitude Journaling. It sounds fancy, right? But really, it's just taking a few minutes out of your day to jot down things you're grateful for. Imagine this as a daily nudge to stop comparing yourself to others. Instead of scrolling through social media and feeling like you're in last place in the life race, focus inward. Write about what makes you unique and extraordinary. Even if it's as simple as "I'm thankful for my ability to fry an egg perfectly," that's gold! This self-reflection transitions your mind from external accolades to the beauty of internal values. Studies have shown that journaling can significantly enhance overall well-being by focusing on positive experiences (Oppland, 2017).

Now, let's take a trip into the land of imagination with Gratitude Visualizations. Picture those moments when you've felt genuinely proud of yourself—like when you nailed that presentation at work or finished a workout despite wanting to snooze in bed all morning. These imagined scenarios are powerful. By visualizing these moments, you foster deep self-acceptance. It's like giving yourself a high-five in your mind, reinforcing the idea that you are enough, no strings attached.

Speaking of high-fives, let's talk about Thanking Yourself. No, seriously—try saying "thank you" to yourself out loud or in your head. Maybe it sounds cheesy, but verbal expressions of gratitude directed at oneself can work wonders. Think about it: We often wait for others to acknowledge our achievements, but why not cut out the middleman? Tell yourself, "Thank you for sticking through that tough meeting," or "Thanks for pushing me to go for a run today." This practice reinforces self-resilience and positivity, helping you to recognize your worth without seeking external validation.

Gratitude Circles bring another dimension to the mix. It's group therapy with a twist—all about sharing and listening. Gather friends or family members and take turns expressing gratitude about experiences or qualities within the circle. This isn't just reserved for Thanksgiving dinner; it's a chance to feel connected and accepted while hearing different perspectives. Hearing someone else being thankful for something you might've overlooked in your life opens your eyes to new ways of seeing the world. The shared nature of these circles amplifies feelings of belonging and acceptance, linking everyone in a community of gratefulness.

Trying these exercises consistently is crucial because it helps establish a habit. Regular gratitude practice has been shown to boost mental well-being, especially during challenging times (Kini et al., 2016). If you're thinking, "This sounds great, but who has the time?" remember, these practices don't require hours. Start small. Spend five minutes before bed writing in your gratitude journal, or dedicate a moment during your morning coffee to visualize your accomplishments. When brushing your teeth, Express thanks to yourself, and plan a monthly virtual gratitude circle with your far-flung friends. You'll notice that with time, giving yourself this space to reflect will nurture self-love naturally.

The Transformative Power of Appreciation

Practicing gratitude for oneself can be a transformative force, providing a foundation of self-compassion that boosts personal growth and confidence. Let's dive into how appreciating oneself can make a significant difference.

Firstly, consider the idea of appreciating progress over perfection. Society often nudges us towards unattainable standards, leaving us perpetually dissatisfied with our achievements. But what if we shifted our perspective? By focusing on progress rather than perfection, we cultivate patience and self-tolerance. For example, imagine someone learning to play the guitar. Initially, their attempts might sound more like a cat trapped in a cello, but each strum and chord learned marks progress. Celebrating these small victories builds resilience against external pressures and teaches us to value our journeys, not just destinations.

This mindset doesn't end with the individual; it has a ripple effect on those around them. When you embrace self-appreciation, others notice and start recognizing their worth. Picture a workplace where everyone exchanges high-fives for completing tasks, no matter how minor. This atmosphere of encouragement fosters a sense of community and mutual appreciation. As you appreciate your growth, you inspire others to see value in their efforts, reinforcing a positive cycle within your surroundings.

Now, let's tackle challenges. It's easy to feel overwhelmed when faced with setbacks. However, self-appreciation allows us to reframe these hurdles as opportunities for growth. Remember the myth of Sisyphus, forever pushing a boulder uphill. Now imagine if he celebrated each inch gained. Challenges become less daunting when approached with a mindset that values every effort and lesson learned. Self-acknowledgment during tough times transforms potential despair into motivation, nurturing resilience and courage to persevere.

On top of this, celebrating one's uniqueness through gratitude can fuel authenticity, empowering individuals to pursue passions and interests. Think of artists who break conventions; their masterpieces reflect their unique perspective. Similarly, embracing what makes you different unlocks creativity and passion that drive personal fulfillment. Gratitude for your quirks and talents allows you to step confidently into roles and pursuits that align with your true self.

The research underscores these benefits. A review of studies suggests that high self-esteem positively influences various life domains, such as relationships, career success, and mental health (Blouin, 2022). While self-esteem isn't a cure-all, even slight boosts in self-appreciation accumulate over time, leading to long-term psychological benefits. Moreover, maintaining high self-esteem is distinct from narcissism—a critical differentiation that ensures we foster healthy self-respect rather than superiority.

How do we practically incorporate self-appreciation into daily life? It could be as simple as maintaining a gratitude journal. Jotting down instances when you've felt proud or grateful for your actions can reinforce positive self-reflection and acceptance. Likewise, being mindful and intentional about thanking yourself—verbally or mentally—reinforces self-encouragement and bolsters confidence. These practices gently remind us of our capabilities and achievements, steering us away from self-doubt.

Finally, engaging in supportive communities where shared gratitude stories can magnify feelings of connection and acceptance. Whether participating in group discussions or simply swapping tales of perseverance, these interactions create spaces where self-appreciation thrives. They remind us that while our journeys are unique, we're not alone in navigating life's challenges. Why do you think AA meetings are so effective at reaffirming sobriety?

Diminishing The Need For External Validation

We often find ourselves tangled in a web of external validation in our quest for self-worth. Social media likes, praises from colleagues at work, and compliments about our appearance can feel like the glue holding us together. But here's a plot twist: gratitude shines a light on the inner qualities that make us unique, reducing our craving for others' approval. It's like having a secret superpower that boosts your resilience every time you remember why you're fabulous.

Imagine if you woke up one morning, looked in the mirror, and loved what you saw—not because someone told you to, but because you've learned to appreciate your quirks, strengths, and weaknesses. Recognizing what you love about yourself makes the opinions of others less impactful. Who knew self-love could be so empowering? By fostering gratitude for what lies within, you become the main character of your own story, unbothered by the side characters who'd criticize your plotline.

Gratitude cultivates authentic self-appreciation that's delightfully independent of judgment. You start appreciating how wonderfully weird you are, perhaps even recognizing that your laugh sounds like a mix between a donkey braying and a musical note. Each acknowledgment chips away at the heavy armor we've donned to protect ourselves from judgment. Over time, this opens up possibilities for living life more freely, such as wearing mismatched socks just because of or choosing to sit with a new friend during lunch without fear of judgment.

Embracing one's flaws through gratitude can enhance emotional resilience and stability. We've all got parts of ourselves we're not ecstatic about—like our tendency to forget names immediately after introductions or maybe a propensity to spill coffee on white shirts. However, embracing these flaws with gratitude transforms them into endearing traits rather than burdens. Suddenly, they're charming anecdotes at parties instead of sources of shame. This acceptance fortifies you against emotional hurricanes; it's hard to get knocked down when you know there's no perfect version of you waiting to be judged.

Let's dive into practical examples to demonstrate how gratitude can uphold internal sources of self-worth. Picture a typical day when someone cuts you off in traffic, an email lands in your inbox with feedback about your latest project, and your pet decides now is the time to vomit on the freshly cleaned carpet. Instead of spiraling into despair or rage, gratitude allows you to pause and see the good. That driver saved you from getting stuck at a longer light, the feedback helps improve a skill, and the floor remains spotless where it counts.

Furthermore, research supports this transformative power of gratitude. Studies have shown that those who actively practice gratitude interventions—such as journaling what they're thankful for or thanking people who made a difference in their lives—are more likely to experience heightened self-esteem (Homan & Tylka, 2018). This makes sense because acknowledging countless aspects of life you value, including your inherent qualities, leaves less room for insecurity or doubt to fester.

Appreciating inner qualities provides emotional nourishment, creating a buffer between you and societal demands. Consider Tom, who spent years seeking approval through professional accolades, only to discover that they faded faster than ice cream on a hot day. When Tom shifted focus inward and acknowledged strengths like kindness and creativity, he noticed two things: his anxiety levels dropped, and he cared less about others' opinions. Now, he smiles at family gatherings where the topic strays to career success, knowing his worth isn't tied to LinkedIn profiles.

Of course, integrating gratitude into everyday routines requires intentionality. It might be setting aside five minutes each morning to reflect on what makes you uniquely you—or an evening ritual where you list three personal successes of the day, whether remembering to water plants or finally mastering that tricky yoga pose. These tiny rituals accumulate into profound shifts over time. Your identity starts rooting itself deeply inside, immune to seasonal winds of external judgment.

The beauty of gratitude is its universal application across various facets of life. Its capacity to foster genuine self-worth grows stronger each time we acknowledge who we are becoming and who we've been. Reflecting on moments where courage carried us through difficult conversations or humor turned awkwardness into laughter embodies genuine appreciation, independent from outside evaluation.

Bringing It All Together

As we wrap up this exploration of gratitude and self-compassion, imagine yourself with those magical glasses of gratitude firmly perched on your nose. You've learned how they can transform grayish life moments into vibrant experiences, all while rewiring your brain to focus on the positive. By practicing small acts like journaling or visualizing past triumphs, you've equipped yourself with a toolkit to fend off pesky external judgments. But it's not just about feeling the warm fuzzies; it's about creating a mindset shift that allows everyday mishaps to become less banana peel and more trampoline—bouncing back instead of slipping away.

Ultimately, nurturing gratitude isn't just about putting a smile on your face. It's about building a sturdy foundation similar to the Great Pyramid of Giza. Then, our bolstered self-love can weather life's occasional coconut storms. Regularly appreciating what's within makes you less likely to be swayed by the harsh opinions orbiting around you. You've now got the secret sauce to live a life where your quirks are celebrated, your strengths are acknowledged, and even your flaws have a rightful place at the table. Remember, you are the main character in your story, and with gratitude as your sidekick, you're ready to face each new chapter with confidence and humor. Best advice, JUST BE YOURSELF!!

ABOUT THE AUTHOR

G.R. Stintzi is a passionate writer and observer of life, drawing on years of real-world insight and research in relationships and self-improvement. A former pre-med student at Washington State University, Stintzi has spent the last five years honing his craft, blending humor with heartfelt reflections. His writing aims to offer readers snippets of encouragement, using relatable experiences to inspire positive change and provide them with encouragement and practical wisdom to navigate their journeys. With the belief that laughter and authenticity can illuminate even the most challenging situations, Gerald is dedicated to helping others navigate their journeys with a lighter heart and a clearer mind. He enjoys connecting with others and exploring life unfiltered when he's not writing.

REFERENCES

Chapter 1 Reference List

Arias, E. (2019, July). How does media influence social norms? A field experiment on the role of common knowledge. *Gender Action Portal.* https://gap.hks.harvard.edu/how-does-media-influence-social-norms-field-experiment-role-com mon-knowledge

Ibrahim, F., Brill, E., Meyberg, T., & Herzberg, P. Y. (2023). The impostor phenomenon in the eye of knowledgeable others: The association of the impostor phenomenon with the judge's accuracy. *Frontiers in Psychology, 14,* 1290686. https://doi.org/10.3389/fpsyg.2023.1290686

Jhangiani, R., & Tarry, H. (2022). The feeling self: Self-esteem. *Principles of Social Psychology – 1st International Edition.* https://opentextbc.ca/socialpsychology/chapter/the-feeling-self-self-esteem/

Ledesma, C. B. (2023, July 20). Societal and cultural influences on relationship expectations.
Medium. https://medium.com/@cecilledesma 20547/societal-and-cultural-influences-on-relationship-exp ectations-ba39d87aaeba

Oksanen, A., Celuch, M., Oksa, R., & Savolainen, I. (2024, August 2). Online communities come with real-world consequences for individuals and societies. *Communications Psychology.* https://doi.org/10.1038/s44271-024-00112-6

Sutton, J. (2019, January 3). What is resilience and why is it important to bounce back? *PositivePsychology.* https://positivepsychology.com/what-is-resilience/

Talisman Wealth Advisor. (2024). Talisman Wealth Advisors. https://www.talismanwealthadvisors.com/the-power-of-emotional-self-reliance

Walker, D. L., & Saklofske, D. H. (2023, January 2). Development, factor structure, and psychometric validation of the impostor phenomenon assessment: A novel assessment of impostor phenomenon. *Assessment.* https://doi.org/10.1177/10731911221141870

Chapter 2 Reference List

Charlie Health. (2024, July 17). Charlie Health. https://www.charliehealth.com/areas-of-care/anxiety/how-to-get-over-embarrassment

GirlTalkHQ. (2024, August 6). Stepping out from the shadows: The journey from shame into self-acceptance. *GirlTalkHQ.* https://www.girltalkhq.com/stepping-out-from-the-shadows-the-journey-from-shame-into-self-acc eptance/

Lonczak, H. (2020, July 8). Humor in psychology: Coping and laughing your woes away. *PositivePsychology.com.* https://positivepsychology.com/humor-psychology/

Pistoia, J. (2022, June 28). Can you use humor as a coping mechanism? *Psych Central.* https://psychcentral.com/lib/humor-as-weapon-shield-and-psychological-salve

Suttie, J. (2017, July 17). How laughter brings us together. *Greater Good.* https://greatergood.berkeley.edu/article/item/how_laughter_brings_us_t ogether

Knill Allen, T. (2024). Using comedy as a coping mechanism. *Redwood Bark.* https://redwoodbark.org/85980/culture/using-comedy-as-a-coping-mechanism/

Why it takes humour to sustain a long-term relationship. (n.d.). *Psyche.* https://psyche.co/ideas/why-it-takes-humour-to-sustain-a-long-term-rela

Chapter 3 Reference List

Empath, an. (2022, October 13). Adventuring with Poseidon. *Adventuring with Poseidon.* https://www.adventuringwithposeidon.com/blog/how-can-an-empath-block-negative-energy

Charlie Health. (2024, April 5). A guide for how to detach from someone. https://www.charliehealth.com/post/how-to-detach-from-someone

Lozano, G. (2024). How to emotionally detach from someone. *Grow Therapy.* https://growtherapy.com/blog/healthy-ways-to-emotionally-detach/

Newman, S. (2016, February 15). How highly sensitive people can shield themselves from negativity. *Psych Central.* https://psychcentral.com/blog/how-sensitive-people-can-shield-themselves-from-negativity

Navigating relationship dynamics: Understanding conflict. (2023). *MyMind - Centre for Mental Wellbeing.* https://mymind.org/relationship-dynamics-1

Pivot Wellness. (2020, April 8). The dreaded drama triangle. *Pivot Wellness.* https://startyourpivot.com/blog/2020/4/8/the-dreaded-drama-trianglenbsp

Theatre of the Absurd: Teaching with drama. (2022, October 13). Lesson: Impossible. https://www.lessonimpossible.com/blog/theatre-of-the-absurd

Lesson: Impossible. (2022, October 13). *Lesson: Impossible.* https://www.lessonimpossible.com/blog/tag/theatre+of+the+absurd

Chapter 4 Reference List

Albalooshi, S., Moeini-Jazani, M., Fennis, B. M., & Warlop, L. (2019, June 11). Reinstating the resourceful self: When and how self-affirmations improve executive performance of the powerless. *Personality and Social Psychology Bulletin.* https://doi.org/10.1177/0146167219853840

Andrade, F. C., Erwin, S., Burnell, K., Jackson, J., Storch, M., Nicholas, J., & Zucker, N. (2023, April 28). Intervening on social comparisons on social media: Electronic daily diary pilot study. *JMIR Mental Health.* https://doi.org/10.2196/42024

Eden, A. L., Johnson, B. K., Reinecke, L., & Grady, S. M. (2020). Media for coping during

COVID-19 social distancing: Stress, anxiety, and psychological well-being. *Frontiers in Psychology, 11,* Article 577639. https://doi.org/10.3389/fpsyg.2020.577639

Moore, C. (2019, March 4). Positive daily affirmations: Is there science behind it? *Positive Psychology.* https://positivepsychology.com/daily-affirmations/

Riopel, L. (2019, January 20). Resilience examples: What key skills make you resilient? *PositivePsychology.com.* https://positivepsychology.com/resilience-skills/

The effects of social media on body image constructs among active women. (2018). *ResearchGate.* https://www.researchgate.net/publication/353224818_The_Effects_of_Social_Media_on_Body_Image_Constructs_Among_Active_Women

Tugade, M. M., & Fredrickson, B. L. (2004). Resilient individuals use positive emotions to bounce back from negative emotional experiences. *Journal of Personality and Social Psychology, 86*(2), 320–333. https://doi.org/10.1037/0022-3514.86.2.320

Vaingankar, J. A. (2022, March 4). Social media–driven routes to positive mental health among youth: Qualitative enquiry and concept mapping study. *JMIR Pediatrics and Parenting.* https://doi.org/10.2196/32758

Chapter 5 Reference List

Chen, S. (2019, March). Authenticity in context: Being true to working selves. *Review of General Psychology.* https://doi.org/10.1037/gpr0000160

Dapkus, W. (2024, May 20). Positive self-talk can transform your life and mindset. *White Oak Institute for Growth and Wellness.* https://whiteoakinstitute.net/blog/achieving-wellness-through-positive-self-talk/

Empower yourself: Tools and techniques for overcoming negative self-talk. (2023, August 8). *OCD.app.*

https://ocd.app/empower-yourself-tools-and-techniques-for-overcoming-negative-self-talk/

Physicians can easily get trapped in the need for external validation. (2021). *Joy in Family Medicine*. https://www.joyinfamilymedicine.com/blog/over-reliance-on-external-validation

Patrick, W. (2021, March 21). The emotional benefits of feeling unique. *Psychology Today*. https://www.psychologytoday.com/us/blog/why-bad-looks-good/202103/the-emotional-benefits-f eeling-unique

Plesa, P. (2023, May 25). Authenticization: Consuming commodified authenticity to become "authentic" subjects. *Theory & Psychology; SAGE Publishing*. https://doi.org/10.1177/09593543231174030

People-pleasing: A breakdown of the bad habit and how to kick it. (2022, April 19). *Thriveworks*. https://thriveworks.com/help-with/self-improvement/people-pleasing/

Sutton, A. (2020, January). Living the good life: A meta-analysis of authenticity and well-being. *International Journal of Wellbeing*. https://doi.org/10.5502/ijw.v10i1.1816

Chapter 6 Reference List

12 benefits of self-esteem (and 10 tips to improve yours). (n.d.). *Indeed Career Guide*. https://www.indeed.com/career-advice/career-development/benefits-of-self-esteem

Dhote, A., & Sinha, A. (2024, April 16). Personality traits and self-acceptance among young adults. *International Journal of Research and Analytical Reviews,* 11(2). https://www.researchgate.net/publication/380547070_Personality_Traits_and_Self_Acceptance_among_young_adults

AlliGee. (2023, November 4). Seizing individuality and embracing non-conformity: The inspiring journey of the Dead Poets Society. *Medium*. https://medium.com/@alligeewriting/seizing-individuality-and-embracing-non-conformity-the-insp iring-journey-of-the-dead-poets-society-fb1da38cba5b

Godwin, J. (2023, March 12). Let's talk about... individuality. *Let's Talk About Mental Health.* https://letstalkaboutmentalhealth.com.au/2023/03/12/individuality/

Pascoe, G. (2023, March 21). The value in finding and using your strengths. *Mentorloop.* https://mentorloop.com/blog/using-your-strengths/

Tibubos, A. N., Köber, C., Habermas, T., & Rohrmann, S. (2019, April). Does self-acceptance captured by life narratives and self-report predict mental health? A longitudinal multi-method approach. *Journal of Research in Personality, 78,* 93-102. https://doi.org/10.1016/j.jrp.2019.01.003

Why nonconformity cures a sick self and a sick society. (2023, August 22). *Academy of Ideas.* https://academyofideas.com/2023/08/why-nonconformity-cures-a-sick-self-and-a-sick-society/

Writer, G. (2024, May 8). Embracing individualism: The power of personal freedom and expression. *Medium.* https://medium.com/illumination/embracing-individualism-the-power-of-personal-freedom-and-ex pr

Chapter 7 Reference List

Bounds, D. (2024, May 10). Social media's impact on our mental health and tips to use it safely.
UC Davis Health.
https://health.ucdavis.edu/blog/cultivating-health/social-medias-impact-our-mental-health-and-tip s-to-use-it-safely/2024/05

Bailey, E. R., Matz, S. C., Youyou, W., & Iyengar, S. S. (2020, October 6). Authentic self-expression on social media is associated with greater subjective well-being. *Nature Communications, 11*(1), 1-13. https://doi.org/10.1038/s41467-020-18539-w

Cifelli, K. (2021, December 2). FAU | Social media and how it affects our self-image. *Florida Atlantic University.* https://www.fau.edu/thrive/students/thrive-thursdays/ourselfimage/index.php

Medium. (n.d.). Social media: The struggle of authenticity vs. acceptance. *Medium.* https://medium.com/mind-cafe/social-media-the-struggle-of-authenticity-vs-acceptance-edf0d1d a4543

Murray, S. (2019, July 8). Yes, social media is a highlight reel—and that's okay. *Verily.* https://verilymag.com/2019/07/social-media-highlight-reel-ok-2019

Moreschi, A. (2022). Social media beauty filters impact on mental health. *WNWO.* https://www.nbc24.com/news/spotlight-on-america/social-media-beauty-filters-impacting-the-me ntal-health-of-young-women-tiktok-meta-snapchat-instagram-university-of-london-study-bold-gla mour-facetune-bodytune-airbrush

Somersall, M. (2022, August 11). Editing out imperfection: Social media's blur between reality and fantasy. *VOX ATL.* https://voxatl.org/editing-out-imperfection-social-medias-blur-between-reality-and-fantasy/

Smith, M. (2023, May 16). The impacts of social media on youth self-image. *Loma Linda University Health.* https://news.llu.edu/health-wellness/impacts-of-social-media-youth-self-image

Chapter 8 Reference List

Ewing, J. (2023, December 28). Salience Health. *Salience Health.* https://saliencehealth.com/news/learn-how-to-say-no-setting-boundaries-for-a-healthier-life/

Moore, M. (2022, September 8). Here's 3 ways boundaries can help you. *Psych Central.* https://psychcentral.com/relationships/the-importance-of-personal-boundaries

On boundaries: A therapist's guide on setting healthy boundaries. (n.d.). *Therapy with Olivia.* https://www.therapywitholivia.com/blog/a-therapists-guide-on-setting-healthy-boundaries Papyrus. (2023, May 12). The importance of setting boundaries and saying no. *Papyrus UK | Suicide Prevention Charity.* https://www.papyrus-uk.org/setting-boundaries/

Selby. (2023, August 22). Establishing healthy boundaries for effective communication skills.
Everyday Speech.
https://everydayspeech.com/blog-posts/general/establishing-healthy-boundaries-for-effective-co mmunication-skills/

The importance of setting boundaries: 10 benefits for you and your relationships. (n.d.).
BetterHelp. https://www.betterhelp.com/advice/general/the-importance-of-setting-boundaries-10-benefits-for -you-and-your-relationships/

Admin. (2023, October 9). How not setting boundaries leads to a compromised mental health.
The New Hope MHCS.
https://www.thenewhopemhcs.com/how-not-setting-boundaries-leads-to-a-compromised-mentalhealth/

Editor. (2023, September 3). Boundary setting in communication: 5 ways to say no with respect.
RCademy. https://rcademy.com/boundary-setting-in-c

Chapter 9 Reference List

A guided meditation for self-love. (n.d.). *Yoga International.*
https://yogainternational.com/article/view/guided-meditation-for-self-love

Eanes, R. (2021, April 14). The myth of self-regulation. *Generation Mindful.* https://genmindful.com/blogs/mindful-moments/the-myth-of-self-regulation

Five common myths about mindfulness: Debunked. (2021, April 19).
WorkLifePsych. https://www.worklifepsych.com/five-common-myths-about-mindfulness-debunked/

Headspace. (2021). The benefits of body scan meditation. *Headspace.*
https://www.headspace.com/meditation/body-scan

Mindful living: Integrating mindfulness meditation into daily life in 6 easy steps. (2024, March 13). *Goddess Women App.*
https://www.goddesswomenapp.com/blog/integrating-mindfulness-meditation/

Mindful staff. (2020, July 8). What is mindfulness? *Mindful.*
https://www.mindful.org/what-is-mindfulness/

Mindfulness myths. (n.d.). *The Wellbeing Collective.*
https://thewellbeingcollective.com/blog/mindfulness-myths

Ashley. (2019, September 10). 6 simple mindfulness techniques you can do anywhere. *Ritu Bhasin.* https://ritubhasin.com/blog/6-simple-mindfulness-techniques-you-can-do-anywhere/

Chapter 10 Reference List

Blog WP. (2024, October 18). *A Blythe Coach.*
https://ablythecoach.com/?page_id=38

DMS Analytics Consulting. (2024, September 16). Joy. *The Red Hand Files.* https://www.theredhandfiles.com/joy/

Hoang, V. (2021, January 7). The humorous, absurd, plural, and defiant story of Generation Z.
Your Majesty Co.
https://yourmajesty.co/article/the-humorous-absurd-plural-and-defiant-story-of-generation-z

Lamothe, C. (2018, June 22). The benefits of laughing at yourself, according to science.
Shondaland. https://www.shondaland.com/live/a21755063/benefits-laughing-at-yourself-self-deprecation-scie nce-psychology/

Pike, M. (2019, August 27). When does self-deprecation become a crutch? *Talkspace.* https://www.talkspace.com/blog/self-deprecation-unhealthy/

The Jed Foundation. (2023). Understanding social comparison on social media. *The Jed Foundation.*
https://jedfoundation.org/resource/understanding-social-comparison-on-social-media/

Warrender, D., & Milne, R. (2020, February 24). How use of social media and social comparison affect mental health. *Nursing Times.*
https://www.nursingtimes.net/news/mental-health/how-use-of-social-media-and-social-comparis on-affect-mental-health-24-02-2020/

What is Gen Z humor? Understanding absurd meme culture. (2024). *Greenlight.* https://greenlight.com/learning-center/parenting-and-family/gen-z-humor

Chapter 11 Reference List

Butterfly, A. L. (2024, February 9). Finding your voice: The power of authentic expression.
Medium.
https://medium.com/@writerbutterfly/finding-your-voice-the-power-of-authentic-expression-095c cc1fe080

Bay. (2024, July 22). Top 10 personal mantra examples to transform your life. *Bay Area CBT Center.* https://bayareacbtcenter.com/personal-mantra/

Darr, C., & Doss, E. (2022). The fake one is the real one: Finstas, authenticity, and context collapse in teen friend groups. *Journal of Computer-Mediated Communication, 27*(3), 183-199. https://doi.org/10.1093/jcmc/zmac009

GirlTalkHQ. (2023, September 7). How I navigated the tumultuous waters of self-discovery to find empowerment & my unique voice. *GirlTalkHQ.*
https://www.girltalkhq.com/how-i-navigated-the-tumultuous-waters-of-self-discovery-to-find-emp owerment-my-unique-voice/

Luxe Femme Chronicles. (2024, August 15). How to cultivate self-love and confidence. *Medium.* https://medium.com/@charge.mattress/how-to-cultivate-self-love-and-confidence-fafaeb13c47f

Rewriting the narrative: Empowering beliefs for women. (2024). *Be Brave Enough.*
https://www.becomebraveenough.com/blog/rewriting-the-narrative-empowering-beliefs-for-wom en

Santer, N., Manago, A., & Bleisch, R. (2022, May 19). Narratives of the self in polymedia contexts: Authenticity and branding in Generation Z. *Qualitative Psychology, 9*(2), 215-230. https://doi.org/10.1037/qup0000232

View. (2015, October 25). Writing mantras for the new school year: Part of #TWTBlog's Throwback Week. *Two Writing Teachers.*

https://twowritingteachers.org/2015/10/25/writing-mantras-for-the-new-school-year-part-of-twtblo gs-throwback-week/

Chapter 12 Reference List

Blouin, M. (2022, April 15). Research review shows self-esteem has long-term benefits. *UC Davis.* https://www.ucdavis.edu/curiosity/news/research-review-shows-self-esteem-has-long-term-bene fits

Drummond, J. (2023, September 15). Why self-confidence is crucial in everyday life. *Jenn Drummond.* https://jenndrummond.com/blog/why-self-confidence-is-crucial-in-everyday-life/

Flayton, L. (2018, November 21). Is gratitude good for your health? *NewYork-Presbyterian.* https://healthmatters.nyp.org/is-gratitude-good-for-your-health/

Gratitude and mental health. (2022, November 17). *Oregon Counseling.* https://oregoncounseling.com/article/gratitude-and-mental-health/

Homan, K. J., & Tylka, T. L. (2018, June). Development and exploration of the gratitude model of body appreciation in women. *Body Image, 26,* 1-10. https://doi.org/10.1016/j.bodyim.2018.01.008
Inge, C. (2018, November 8). 222 gratitude journal prompts for living a life of gratitude. *Human Design with Christie Inge.* https://christieinge.com/gratitude-journal-prompts/

Norberto Eiji Nawa, & Yamagishi, N. (2024, March 7). Distinct associations between gratitude, self-esteem, and optimism with subjective and psychological well-being among Japanese individuals. *BMC Psychology, 12*(1), 1-11. https://doi.org/10.1186/s40359-024-01606-y

Oppland, M. (2017, April 28). 13 most popular gratitude exercises & activities. *PositivePsychology.com.* https://positivepsychology.com/gratitude-exercises/

Chapter 13 Reference List

Bay. (2024, August 8). *Top 10 manipulation tactics and how to counter them.* Bay Area CBT Center. https://bayareacbtcenter.com/top-10-manipulation-tactics-and-how-to-counter-them/

Novak, J. M. (2023, January 23). *How to set healthy boundaries: An act of self-love.* Believe and Create. https://believeandcreate.com/setting-boundaries-healthy-self-love/

Retreat In the Pines. (2023). *Self love is setting boundaries.* Retreat In the Pines. https://retreatinthepines.com/post/dare-to-set-boundaries

Whieldon, L. (2023, November 25). *Manipulative relationships.* Reconnect Counseling. https://www.reconnectcounseling.com/unhealthy-relationship-patterns-categorizing-the-21-types /manipulative-relationships/

www.ingramcontent.com/pod-product-compliance
Lightning Source LLC
Chambersburg PA
CBHW050221270326
41914CB00003BA/512